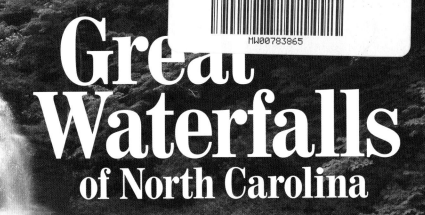

# Great Waterfalls
## of North Carolina

**A GUIDE FOR HIKERS, PHOTOGRAPHERS, AND WATERFALL ENTHUSIASTS**

# Neil Regan

**Parkway Publishers, Inc.**
**Boone, North Carolina**

**Photographs and text copyright © 2010 by Neil Regan**
**All rights reserved**

**Suggested Cataloging Data based on a Previous Edition**

Regan, Neil.
Great Waterfalls of North Carolina: A Guide for Hikers,
Photographers, and Waterfall Enthusiasts / by Neil Regan.

x, 150 p. : col. ill. ; 22 cm.
9781933251707 (pbk.)
Includes index.
Waterfalls --North Carolina.
GB1425.N8 R33 2010
551.48/409756 22

2008908243

*Book design by Aaron Burleson, spokesmedia*

PRINTED IN CHINA

**This work
is dedicated to:**

# My Mother
*Soaring with the angels, I miss you so much.*

# My Father
*The best man I know.*

# My Sister
*I couldn't ask for a better one.*

*And*

# My Good Friends
*Thanks for being there.*

# Acknowledgements

I would like to thank the following individuals and organizations
for their valuable contributions to this work.

Jack and Emily Smathers
First Peak Visitor Center of Columbus, NC
The Members of the Tryon Garden Club, Tryon, NC
Adolph Atkins at Atkins Orchards Produce, Saluda, NC
Top of the Falls Realty, Brevard, NC
Living Waters Ministry, Balsam Grove, NC
William Dinkins, Eastatoe Falls owner, Rosman, NC
The Park Rangers at the Visitors Center, Pisgah National Forest
Park Ranger James Ledgerwood, Gorges State Park
Ed Fortag, US Forest Service, Black Mountain Campground
John Hunnicutt, Cooper Creek Trout Farm, Bryson City, NC
Jerry, Gennie, and Cameron Cauthen

And especially Rao Aluri at Parkway Publishers and Aaron Burleson at spokesmedia

# Foreword

What makes a waterfall great? There are many characteristics that contribute to a waterfall's greatness. Height, width, water flow, surrounding environment, history, and overall appearance are some of them. Greatness in a waterfall can vary from the biggest, like Whitewater Falls and Rainbow Falls near Sapphire, to smaller and lesser-known examples like Big Laurel Falls near Franklin or Toms Creek Falls near Marion. The ultimate judges of a waterfall are the individuals that make the effort to find and view it. Obviously, I consider all of the falls I have presented here to be great. I hope that you will agree.

There are hundreds of waterfalls and cascades in the North Carolina mountains. Not all of these are necessarily noteworthy or deserving of being included here. There are other waterfalls that I would consider great that are not included. Some are in such remote locations that they are impossible to reach except maybe by helicopter. Other great waterfalls are located on privately owned land and are not open to the public. There are a number of generous and accommodating property owners who welcome visitors, such as the owners of Eastatoe Falls in Rosman, Birdrock Falls and Mill Shoals in Balsam Grove, and Pearsons Falls in Tryon. Shunkawauken Falls near Columbus is actually split by a public road and would be difficult to post off limits to visitors. There are other owners that do not allow access for their own reasons. I will not send you anywhere that you are not welcome and could be run off or possibly be charged with trespassing. Some are in locations that are dangerous to try to reach, and in good conscience I would not send you somewhere that there is a good chance you would be injured. Having said that, there are inherent dangers when you are exploring in mostly undeveloped wilderness areas. There are black bears and poisonous snakes here that you need to be aware of. After all, this is their home and we are simply visitors. Many trails have some areas that could cause injury if you are not careful. Simply be aware of your surroundings and keep your eyes open for any type of danger while you are in any wilderness setting. Many of the trails that lead to these falls are along old logging roads. This region was logged extensively in the late 1800's and early 1900's. What was then a scourge on the beauty of the land is now a benefit for hikers, mountain bikers, photographers, and waterfall enthusiasts. Many of these falls would be much harder or nearly impossible to reach without the network of old roads that serve as the foundation for the trail system that we have today.

For more comprehensive listings of waterfalls in the North Carolina mountains check out the book, *North Carolina Waterfalls* by Kevin Adams (John F. Blair, 2005) or Rich Stevenson's website, www. ncwaterfalls.com. Both are great resources that I have found to be quite invaluable.

I have done my very best to give you detailed descriptions, specific directions, and accurate ratings for the falls and trails in this book. I have compiled these facts the old-fashioned way, by going to each of them and recording as accurately as I can, the information that I have presented here. It is my sincere hope that this guide will not only assist you in finding and photographing the wonderful array of great waterfalls this region has to offer, but will also provide you with opportunities for fantastic hikes and rewarding experiences in one of the most beautiful areas of the world. For questions, comments, or to order signed copies, please email me at neil.regan@yahoo.com. I sincerely thank you for your interest in this book and wish you the very best of luck, beautiful weather, and safe travels.

# The Photographs

The photographs presented in this book are entirely my own. You will notice that I prefer to use a fast shutter speed to photograph these falls, freezing the water and preserving more detail. I have always preferred this approach, though some photographers achieve the "velvety" look by using slower shutter speeds. It is simply a matter of personal preference as either approach can produce great pictures.

I have tried to extend to you the benefit of my experience as to the best locations in which to photograph each fall, but you may find more desirable locations depending on your tastes and experience. You must know, however, that the worst and most dangerous location to photograph a waterfall is from the top. None of my photographs was taken there, and with good reason. Every year there are a number of visitors to this region who are either killed or sustain serious injuries from falling off of or being swept over waterfalls. I would strongly caution you against getting near the edge at the top of any waterfall.

The best weather for hiking and viewing waterfalls may be bright sunny days, but they usually produce the worst conditions to actually photograph them. Sunlight reflects off of the water, producing a wicked glare that will ruin a picture. Overcast days are generally the best for photographing falls.

# The Ratings

## Waterfall Beauty Ratings

I have tried to be as objective as I could be in assigning beauty ratings to these waterfalls based on their merits. I considered size, height, water flow, appearance, and surroundings to arrive at a rating for each fall. The "wow" factor was significant as well. If I thought, "Wow, this is a great waterfall" upon seeing it for the first time, then I included it here. Since the 1-10 scale is simple and easy to understand, it was the obvious choice. I have not included any waterfalls that didn't rate at least a 5.

## Trail Difficulty Ratings

The trail difficulty ratings are based on several factors. I considered the length and condition of the trail, grade (steepness), and obstacles such as creek crossings, roots, rocks, and deadfall. Again, the 1-10 scale is used here with a 1 being roadside viewing or a very short easy walk, and a 10 assigned to the trails that only the most serious and skilled hikers should attempt.

# Mileage and Directions

## Mileage

I relied on the digital odometer on my vehicle to record driving distances. As odometers will vary from vehicle to vehicle, use the distances provided as a general guide. Your vehicle's mileage reading may differ slightly from mine.

## Directions

I have attempted to provide you with the simplest and most concise directions that I could to make your journey to each waterfall as easy as possible. I approached this as though I knew nothing about the areas I was traveling to, and tried to give only essential and important details without unnecessary and confusing information.

# Table of Contents

# Waterfalls Location Map

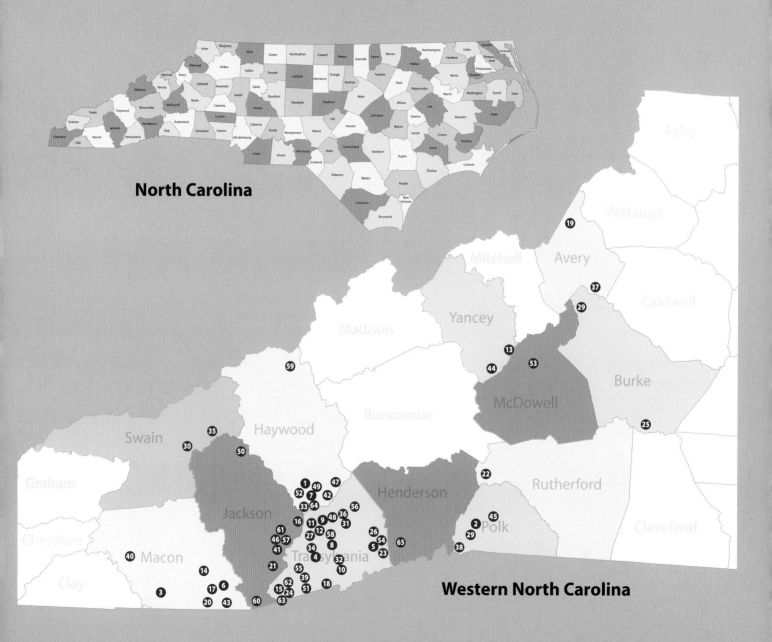

North Carolina

Western North Carolina

# Waterfalls Location Key & Index

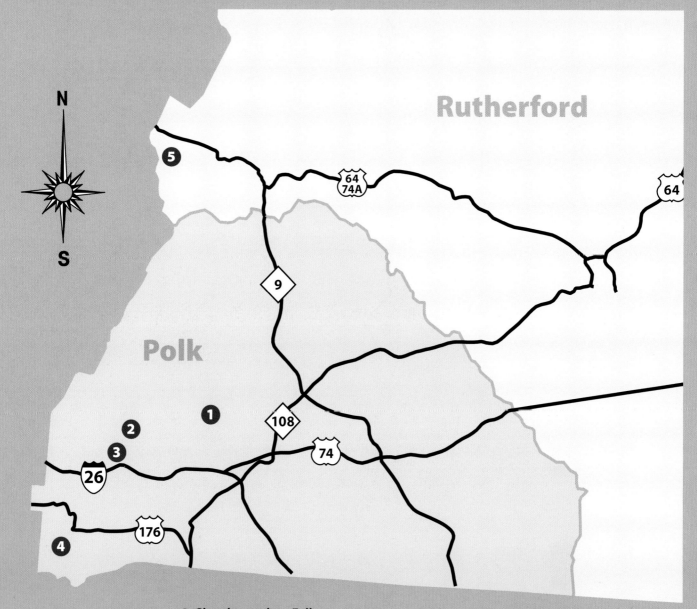

**Rutherford**

**Polk**

1. Shunkawauken Falls
2. Big Bradley Falls
3. Little Bradley Falls
4. Pearsons Falls
5. Hickory Nut Falls

# CHAPTER 1

# Polk County, Chimney Rock Park

*Shunkawauken Falls*

*Big Bradley Falls*

*Little Bradley Falls*

*Pearsons Falls*

*Hickory Nut Falls*

# Shunkawauken Falls
## (Horse Creek Falls)

**Beauty:** 7

**Water Flow:** Small

**Height:** Several hundred feet total

**Type:** A long fall with a series of cascades and short falls

**Property Owner:** Private

**County:** Polk

**Trail Rating:** 1, 8 to bottom

**Trail Length (one-way):** Roadside view 0.1 mile; 100 yards to base

**Description:** This is one of the most unique waterfalls in this region. It is very tall and is separated by White Oak Mountain Road giving it the appearance of two totally different falls. The upper section is a long freefall while the lower section below the road is a series of short falls and cascades. Another unique feature is that the falls are near the top of the mountain, whereas most waterfalls in this region are located at much lower elevations.

This fall was called Horse Creek Falls until 1891 when it was renamed for a local Indian chief, hence the unusual name.

**Directions to Trail:** From Mills Street (Hwy 108) in Columbus, turn north on Houston Road (S.R. 1137) and proceed 0.5 miles, bearing right at the fork to stay on Houston Rd. After an additional 0.6 miles on Houston Rd., turn left onto White Oak Mountain Road (S.R. 1136). The falls are located 2.1 miles on the right, the pullout is 2.0 miles on the left.

**Trail Directions:** The trail begins at the pullout and goes very steeply downhill. There are roots and a number of large rocks to negotiate so you will need to be extremely careful should you decide to take this trail.

**Photographic Locations:** It is difficult to photograph the entire waterfall except for late fall, winter, or early spring when the trees are mostly bare. This leaves two different possibilities for shooting this fall. The top section of the fall can be shot from beside the roadway, which is the best location, but be careful of the traffic. The bottom section can be shot from the creek bed near the base, but there is a lot of trash and deadfall here and views are very limited. Care must be used to shoot from here if you choose to.

# Big Bradley Falls
## *(Bradley Falls)*

**Beauty:** 8

**Water Flow:** Small

**Height:** Approximately 100 feet

**Type:** Long fall and small cascades

**Property Owner:** NC Wildlife Resources Commission

**County:** Polk

**Trail Rating:** 5, 10 to base

**Trail Length (one-way):** 0.9 mile

**Description:** This is a spectacular waterfall composed of a long fall and small cascades into pools at the bottom. There are other thin falls and cascades whose size depends on water flow level.

**Directions to Trail:** From I-26 take the Saluda exit (Exit 59) and drive east on Holbert Cove Road (S.R. 1142) for 3.2 miles to a large pullout on the left.

**Trail Directions:** There is an orange gate at the start of the trail. Trail will fork after several yards and you can take either one as they both lead to a logging road that you will take to the right until you reach Cove Creek. Cross the creek either by wading or rock hopping and continue on the road for approximately 0.5 mile. You will pass a steep trail on the left with white painted makings on a large pine tree. This trail leads to the top of the falls so avoid this one. Also pass the next two trails, which are very dangerous trails, including a 20-foot sheer cliff, leading to the bottom. Take the fourth trail on the left for approximately 150 yards that leads down to the edge of the gorge.

**Photographic Locations:** The only relatively safe location to photograph this waterfall is from the edge of the gorge above the fall. Even here you must be careful not to get too close to the edge, as there is a long sheer drop sure to cause serious injury at least. I would strongly caution you to stay away from the top of the falls, as there are people who fall from there every year, resulting in death or critical injury. I wouldn't even consider trying to reach the bottom unless you're an accomplished climber, hence the difficulty rating of 10.

# Little Bradley Falls

**Beauty:** 7

**Water Flow:** Small

**Height:** 40 feet

**Type:** Multi-tiered freefalls

**Property Owner:** NC Wildlife Resources Commission

**County:** Polk

**Trail Rating:** 6

**Trail Length (one-way):** 0.7 mile

**Description:** This is a fantastic waterfall with several tiers of freefalls and small cascades. It is bordered by trees and flows into a shallow pool surrounded by boulders. Flow will vary depending on recent rainfall. With a larger flow it is stunning, but even with a light flow it is still a nice one.

**Directions to Trail:** See Directions for Big Bradley Falls. From the Big Bradley Falls trailhead, continue across the culvert and park in the small dirt pullout on the right.

**Trail Directions:** Trail begins at the pullout and immediately forks. Take the left trail up the bank and proceed to the right on an old logging road. If you take the right fork, you will end up with a wicked bank scramble that leads up to the same logging road anyway. Continue to follow the road and take the right trail at the next fork. At the third fork, again take the right trail down to a small creek crossing. There are red blazes on the trees along this part of the trail. Pick up the logging road across the creek and continue until you come to a crossing at Cove Creek. You can either make a barefoot crossing here to cool your feet or make your way several yards downstream where there are several locations to make a dry crossing on the rocks. Pick up the logging road on the other side as it goes left and ascends gradually. Trail continues until a fork at a pair of stone fireplaces at an old homestead on the left, again take the trail on the right. Continue until you come to another small creek crossing, at this point you will hear the falls ahead and to the left. After crossing, the trail bypasses a campsite and comes out at the pool below the falls.

**Photographic Locations:** Anywhere around the pool on the large rocks would make a good location for excellent photos. The end of the trail makes a good location if you want to include the large rocks in the foreground.

# Pearsons Falls

**Beauty:** 8

**Water Flow:** Moderate

**Height:** Approximately 90 feet

**Type:** Staircase falls and cascades

**Property Owner:** Tryon Garden Club

**County:** Polk

**Trail Rating:** 4

**Trail Length (one-way):** 0.3 mile

**Description:** This is a beautiful medium-sized waterfall with a strong flow that drops down a natural staircase with short falls and cascades. It is an instant favorite for nearly everyone who comes to see it.

The waterfall and surrounding area are owned by the Tryon Garden Club. They do a magnificent job of maintaining the trails and grounds, and a small, tax-deductible admission fee helps with the upkeep. There are picnic areas, benches along the trail, an educational garden, and even porta-johns to use should nature call. Falls are open Tuesday to Saturday, and Wednesday to Saturday in winter. Call (828) 749-3031 for more information.

The falls are named for Charles William Pearson. He is credited with discovering the falls while surveying a possible railroad route from Asheville, NC to Spartanburg, SC shortly after the War Between the States.

**Directions to Trail:** From I-26, take either the Saluda (Exit 59) or Columbus/Tryon exit. From the Saluda exit take Ozone Drive 1.1 miles to NC 176. Turn right, go 0.2 mile to Pearsons Falls Road (S.R. 1102) on the left. Entrance is 2.7 miles on right.

From the Columbus/Tryon exit (Exit 67), take NC 108 west 2.5 miles to Harmon Field Road that branches right. Watch for the "To NC 176" sign. Continue for 0.7 mile to a right on NC 176. Take NC 176 north for 3.8 miles to a left on Pearsons Falls Road. Entrance gate is 1 mile on left.

**Trail Directions:** From the parking area, walk past the rock walled picnic shelter and kiosk and pick up the trail. The trail follows the creek to the base of the falls, with a great stone bridge and some nice cascades to admire.

**Photographic Locations:** There are several good locations for photographing this fall, from a sitting area just downstream, to several viewing areas around the base. Horizontal and vertical shots work well.

# Hickory Nut Falls

**Beauty:** 8

**Water Flow:** Very small

**Height:** Park brochure lists 404 feet

**Type:** Narrow, nearly vertical cascade with short lower falls

**Property Owner:** North Carolina State Parks

**County:** Rutherford

**Trail Rating:** 3 to base, 8 to top

**Trail Length (one-way):** 0.75 mile to base or top, loop trails are 1.5 miles

**Description:** Hickory Nut Falls is a very tall, narrow, nearly vertical cascade with lower short freefalls that flow over a huge exposed cliff face. The height of the main falls has been the topic of great debate nearly since its discovery and is most certainly not as tall as it is advertised to be. Regardless of its actual height, this majestic waterfall is still easily one of the highest in the state and well worth the effort to see it.

The Skyline Trail above the falls was used as a shooting location for the final fight scenes in the movie, *The Last of the Mohicans.*

When in the area, Chimney Rock Park should be high on your list of places to see. There are miles of trails to hike, some of the most beautiful mountain scenery anywhere in the Appalachians, incredible rock formations, a nature center and animal discovery center, a climbing tower, and even rock climbing lessons for the kids. Call (800) 277-9611 or visit chimneyrockpark.com for information.

**Directions to Trail:** Chimney Rock Park is located on US 64/74A between Bat Cave and Lake Lure. The stone gate at the entrance is easy to spot. Cross the bridge and follow the paved road to the ticket plaza.

**Trail Directions:** Hickory Nut Falls Trail begins just below lower parking lot and ascends gradually to observation deck at base of falls. Skyline/Cliff Trail begins either just past Cliff Dwellers Gift Shop at upper parking area or at the Sky Lounge Gift Shop and Deli if you choose to take the elevator and begin there. Visitors to the park are given a brochure with detailed maps.

**Photographic Locations:** Lower falls can be photographed from the base but you can't get all of the falls in a picture from here. The best location to capture the entire fall is from Inspiration Point.

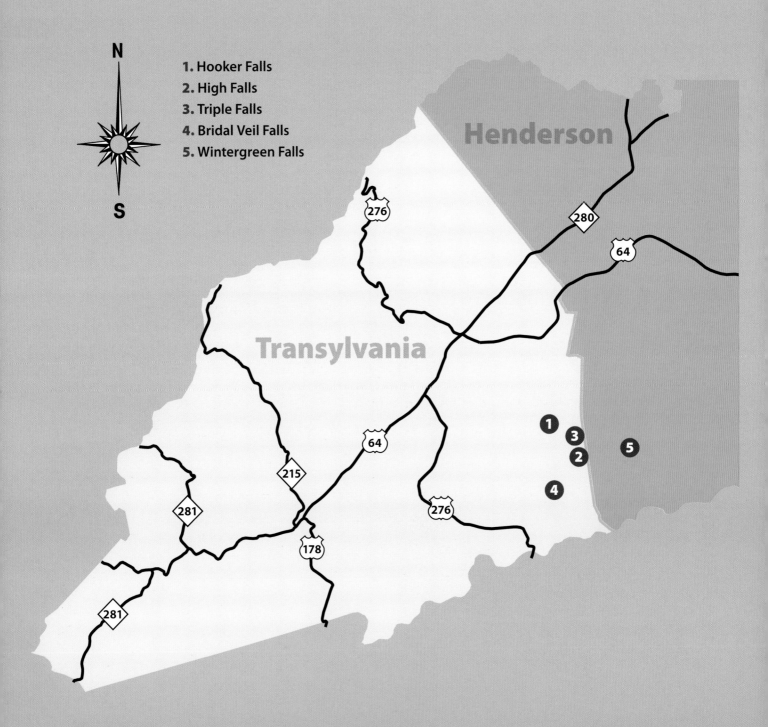

1. Hooker Falls
2. High Falls
3. Triple Falls
4. Bridal Veil Falls
5. Wintergreen Falls

N

S

Henderson

Transylvania

276
280
64
64
215
281
281
178
276

1
3
2
5
4

# CHAPTER 2

# DuPont State Forest

*Hooker Falls*

*High Falls*

*Triple Falls*

*Bridal Veil Falls*

*Wintergreen Falls*

# Hooker Falls
## *(Mill Shoals)*

**Beauty:** 8

**Water Flow:** Large

**Height:** 12 feet

**Type:** Wide freefall

**Property Owner:** DuPont State Forest

**County:** Transylvania

**Trail Rating:** 3

**Trail Length (one-way):** 0.3 mile

**Description:** This is an outstanding example of a wide, short waterfall. It has a large water flow over it most of the year that drops into a huge pool at the base. It is common to see people fishing and swimming here, as well as just sitting and enjoying the environment or having a picnic.

Hooker Falls was previously called Mill Shoals but was renamed for Edmund Hooker. He operated a mill at the falls in the late 1800's. This was one of the falls used as a location in the film, *The Last of the Mohicans,* for the scenes where the canoes go over the falls.

**Directions to Trail:** From Brevard at the intersection of NC 280, US 276, and US 64, take US 64 east for 3.6 miles to a right on Crab Creek Road (S.R. 1528) at the Penrose community. Take Crab Creek Road for 4.3 miles to a right on DuPont Road (S.R. 1259). Drive 3.2 miles to a large parking area for Hooker Falls on the right just before the bridge over the Little River. There is a sign pointing the way just before you get there. Incidentally, DuPont Road becomes Staton Road at the Henderson/Transylvania County line.

**Trail Directions:** The trail starts at the parking area and will fork shortly after. Stay to the left, following the river on Hooker Falls Trail. You will come to the overlook first, while the base is only a short walk to the end of the trail.

**Photographic Locations:** This waterfall can be nicely photographed in profile from a small deck overlook or from the rocks on the left side of the falls, or directly in front from the edge of the large pool at the base.

# High Falls
## (Great Falls, Minnehaha Falls)

**Beauty:** 9

**Water Flow:** Large

**Height:** Approximately 100 feet

**Type:** A series of short falls and long cascades

**Property Owner:** DuPont State Forest

**County:** Transylvania

**Trail Rating:** 3

**Trail Length (one-way):** 0.6 mile

**Description:** This massive and majestic waterfall consists of a series of short falls and cascades that split into several flows at the top. These flow over a huge exposed rock face and into a large rocky pool at the bottom. There is a covered wooden bridge at the top that can be accessed on Buck Forest Road.

High Falls was one of several falls along the Little River to be used as a shooting location in the major Hollywood film, *The Last of the Mohicans.*

**Directions to Trail:** Same as Hooker Falls. From the Hooker Falls parking area turn right on Staton Road and travel 0.9 mile to the Buck Forest Access Area on the left. Park here.

**Trail Directions:** There is a kiosk with trail directions for High Falls and Triple Falls just past the gate on Buck Forest Road that forms the beginning of the trail to reach both falls. Take Buck Forest Road for 0.4 miles to Triple Falls Trail on left. The trail forks almost immediately and you will need to go right on the High Falls Trail for 0.2 mile to the viewing area.

**Photographic Locations:** The Forest Service has done an excellent job of creating a clear viewing area at an obvious spot along the trail. Excellent photographs can be taken here or from the overlook just up the hill behind the trail. A set of steps leads to this location. There is an old stone fireplace here that is all that remains of the Buck Forest Lodge, a popular destination in the mid 1800's.

# Triple Falls
## *(Rag Falls)*

**Beauty:** 9

**Water Flow:** Large

**Height:** A total of approximately 100 feet

**Type:** A three-tiered series of falls and cascades

**Property Owner:** DuPont State Forest

**County:** Transylvania

**Trail Rating:** 4

**Trail Length (one-way):** 0.9 mile from High Falls

**Description:** A spectacular waterfall consisting of three separate tiers of cascades and short falls, hence the name Triple Falls. It was called Rag Falls in the late 1800's, a rather unflattering name for such a beautiful waterfall.

This waterfall is another of several along the Little River to be featured in the major film, *The Last of the Mohicans.* The scenes where the actors walked along a flat rock ledge beside the falls were shot here.

**Directions to Trail:** Same as High Falls.

**Trail Directions:** From High Falls, backtrack 0.1 mile and go left on Triple Falls Trail. Proceed for 0.7 mile to a right turn that will keep you on Triple Falls Trail. Viewing area is 0.1 mile past the turn. Just past viewing area is a trail to the left that will take you down to large flat rock ledges beside the falls.

**Photographic Locations:** The viewing area along the trail is the best location to photograph the entire fall. There is also a covered picnic shelter just above and behind the trail that makes another good location for pictures. You can get closer shots of the upper sections from the flat ledges beside the falls. If you want closer shots of the bottom you can access this area by taking smaller trails downstream and working your way up the riverbed.

# Bridal Veil Falls

**Beauty:** 7

**Water Flow:** Moderate

**Height:** Approximately 120 feet

**Type:** Short free falls with very long cascades

**Property Owner:** DuPont State Forest

**County:** Transylvania

**Trail Rating:** 4 to base, 6 to upper falls

**Trail Length (one-way):** 2 miles

**Description:** A stunning collection of a short, wide free fall with an overhang at the top and very long cascades and short falls at the bottom. All this occurs on a massive rock face that's been carved and pot-holed by water over many centuries.

This fall was also featured in the film, *The Last of the Mohicans,* where the scenes of the actors walking behind the falls were shot. The dialogue scenes behind the falls were actually shot at a soundstage constructed in a warehouse in Asheville, NC. You can crouch and move around behind the falls, but there's not enough clearance to stand up.

**Directions to Trail:** From Hooker Falls or Buck Forest Access Areas, take Staton Road south to the T intersection at Cascade Lake Road. Go left for 2.4 miles and take a left on Reasonover Road. The Fawn Lake Access Area is 2.7 miles on left.

From the downtown area of Brevard, take US 276 South for approximately 10.5 miles to a left on Cascade Lake Road. and an immediate right on Reasonover Road. The Fawn Lake Access Area is 2.7 miles on left.

**Trail Directions:** Trail begins at a kiosk at Reasonover Creek Road. which you will take to the right, go under the power lines, and bear left on Conservation Road. Stay on this road until you get to Shortcut Trail that you can take or go left on Conservation Road., as both come out at an old airstrip. Continue on Conservation Road. until you get to Bridal Veil Falls Road. on the left. Take this road until it ends at a gravel culdesac, where the trail continues several hundred yards down to the falls.

**Photographic Locations:** Anywhere around the upper falls is good and can be accessed by a trail up the left side of the falls. Be careful of the wet areas on the rock face as they are extremely slippery. There are good spots around the base to shoot the cascades and small falls but be careful of snakes here.

# Wintergreen Falls

**Beauty:** 6

**Water Flow:** Small

**Height:** 20 feet

**Type:** Short upper falls, a sliding cascade, and a short lower chute

**Property Owner:** DuPont State Forest

**County:** Henderson

**Trail Rating:** 5

**Trail Length (one way):** 1.5 miles

**Description:** If you want to get away from the crowds while exploring the Dupont waterfalls, this is the place for you. You will likely have this fall all to yourself most of the time. While it is certainly not the biggest fall in the area, it is still a nice find. Short upper falls drop down a steep sliding cascade and flow out a chute at the bottom into a small pool. If you are here during early June, you will catch the rhododendrons in bloom, adding to the beautiful surrounding scenery.

**Directions to Trail:** Beginning at the intersection of US 276, US 64, and NC 280 in Pisgah Forest, take US 64 east for 3.7 miles to a right turn on Crab Creek Road (SR 1528) at Penrose. Continue for 4.3 miles to a right turn on Dupont Road (SR 1259) and go 0.8 mile to a left turn on Sky Valley Road (SR 1260). At 0.9 mile the pavement ends and the road becomes gravel. Continue for 0.7 mile to the Guion Farm Access area on the right.

**Trail Directions:** There is a kiosk at the access area with an area map and information brochures. The trails begin on either side of the kiosk along the tree lines. Both will lead you to Tarkiln Branch Road that you will take for 0.8 mile to Wintergreen Falls Trail that turns left. There is a sign here. At 0.5 mile Sandy Trail forks to the right but keep straight. As you near the creek downstream from the falls, there are trails that branch left and right. Do not take them. You will notice that some helpful park personnel have cut small trees and laid them across the trails so you won't go the wrong way. At the creek the trail turns left and ascends. Stay to the left as the trail follows the creek. The trail takes you over some boulders and roots that you will need to negotiate to get to the falls.

**Photographic Locations:** Anywhere around the pool at the base makes for a good location depending on the types of shots you want. You will be shooting mostly from the boulders gathered around the pool. Horizontal or vertical shots work well here, as do both frontal and profile views.

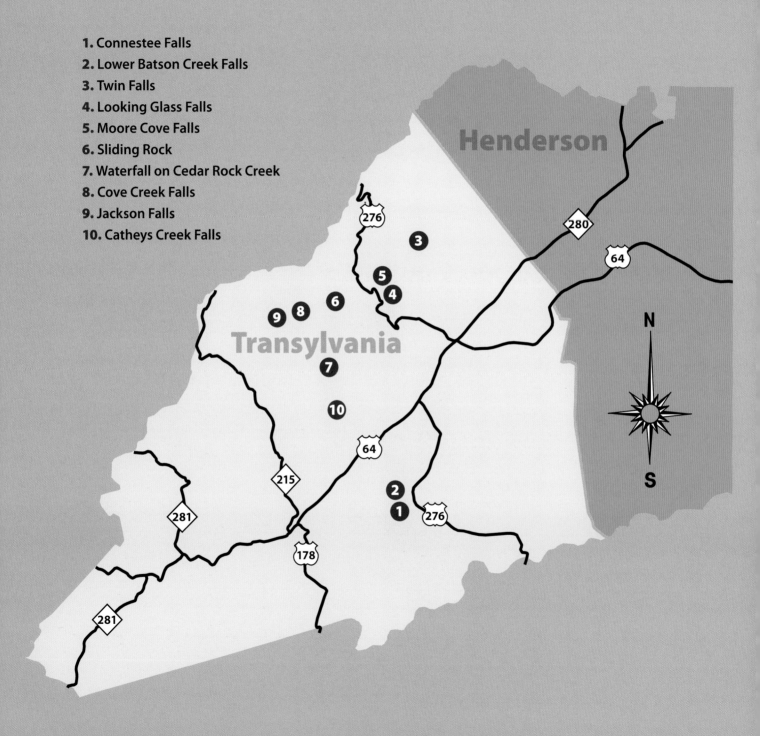

1. Connestee Falls
2. Lower Batson Creek Falls
3. Twin Falls
4. Looking Glass Falls
5. Moore Cove Falls
6. Sliding Rock
7. Waterfall on Cedar Rock Creek
8. Cove Creek Falls
9. Jackson Falls
10. Catheys Creek Falls

Henderson

Transylvania

N

S

# CHAPTER 3

# Brevard, Pisgah National Forest

*Connestee Falls*

*Lower Batson Creek Falls*

*Twin Falls*

*Looking Glass Falls*

*Moore Cove Falls*

*Sliding Rock*

*Waterfall on Cedar Rock Creek*

*Cove Creek Falls*

*Jackson Falls*

*Catheys Creek Falls*

# Connestee Falls

**Beauty:** 7

**Water Flow:** Moderate

**Height:** Over 100 feet

**Type:** Long free fall with small falls and cascades

**Property Owner:** Private

**County:** Transylvania

**Trail Rating:** 1

**Trail Length (one-way):** 100 yards

**Description:** A long free fall with a number of smaller falls and cascades over a staircase creek bed. Despite the limited view, Connestee Falls remains a remarkably beautiful waterfall in a stunning setting. I cannot think of a more impressive location to visit anywhere in region.

The falls are named for a heartbroken Indian princess who, as legend has it, jumped to her death from the top of the falls. There seems to be no evidence that the story is anything but a legend. The falls did receive a beautiful and interesting name, however, regardless of whether the tale is true or not.

**Directions to Trail:** From the downtown area of Brevard take US 276 south for just under 6 miles. There is a large sign on the right for Connestee Falls at Top of the Falls Realty. Turn into this paved parking area and park at the right end of the lot so as not to disrupt business traffic. The owner of this business should be commended for allowing continued access to this property. Not all property owners are so accommodating.

**Trail Directions:** Take the brick path at the right rear of the parking lot next to the creek. Falls are only about 100 yards away.

**Photographic Locations:** The only location to get a picture of this waterfall without trespassing and jumping fences is from the overlook at the top of the falls. If you have access to the Connestee Falls Community, a private, gated residential area, the best shots of this fall are to be taken at the end of a trail on their property. Since most people do not have access, your photographic options are severely limited, as is my rating for this fall. With better views it would be at least an 8.

# Lower Batson Creek Falls
## (Batson Creek Falls)

**Beauty:** 8

**Water Flow:** Moderate

**Height:** over 100 feet

**Type:** Cascades with long free falls

**Property Owner:** Private

**County:** Transylvania

**Trail Rating:** 1

**Trail Length (one-way):** 100 yards

**Description:** A truly spectacular waterfall with upper cascades and long free falls totaling over 100 feet in height. This fall sits opposite Connestee Falls on Carson Creek forming twin falls that flow into the Silver Slip cut and converging into a single creek at the bottom. This is one of the most incredibly beautiful locations I have ever seen.

**Directions to Trail:** Same as Connestee Falls.

**Trail Directions:** Same as Connestee Falls. Separate access to this fall is located in the Connestee Falls Community, which is gated, private, and not accessible to the public. This is not a big hindrance, as the best view is from the Connestee Falls overlook.

**Photographic Locations:** Connestee Falls overlook provides the best and only location for shooting this waterfall.

# Twin Falls

**Beauty:** 7

**Water Flow:** Small

**Height:** Left side falls 80 feet, right side falls 60 feet

**Type:** A series of cascades and free-falls

**Property Owner:** Pisgah National Forest

**County:** Transylvania

**Trail Rating:** 6

**Trail Length (one-way):** 2.0 miles

**Description:** Twin Falls is a set of two different waterfalls separated by a ridge. Each is a series of cascades and free-falls of various heights. You will be rewarded with a great hike and a third waterfall along the way.

**Directions to Trail:** Beginning at the intersection of US 64, US 276, and NC 280 in the town of Pisgah Forest, take US 276 north for 2.2 miles to FR 477 on the right. Take FR 477 for 2.5 miles to a pullout on the right. Park here. You will cross several one-lane bridges and pass the North and South White Pine Group Camps, the Pisgah Forest Riding Stables, and a number of individual campsites on FR 477 before reaching the trailhead.

**Trail Directions:** Buckhorn Gap Trail begins at the pullout and descends moderately into the forest on an old logging road until it reaches Avery Creek. You will pass Waterfall on Avery Creek down to the right at 0.6 mile. Just before you reach the creek, Buckhorn Gap Trail turns left and begins to follow the creek upstream. From this point on there are a few things to remember to make the hike to the falls easy. When in doubt, go upstream. Whenever you come to a horse ford across the creek, there will also be a log footbridge nearby to make a dry crossing. Follow the orange blazes, signs, and orange arrows to continue in the right direction. Stay on Buckhorn Gap Trail for 1.7 miles to Twin Falls Trail on the left where there is a trail marker. This trail will pass a campsite on the right and then ascend up some earth and timber steps, passing through a fallen tree that has been cut away to allow passage. The trail crosses downstream from the left side falls and continues to the right around the ridge to the right side falls.

**Photographic Locations:** Along the paths downstream from both falls make the best locations for photographs here. Shooting at different spots will open up different areas of the upper falls, as there is some vegetation to contend with. You can also shoot Waterfall on Avery Creek while here by taking a visible side path along Buckhorn Gap Trail.

# Looking Glass Falls

**Beauty:** 8

**Water Flow:** Moderate

**Height:** 60 feet

**Type:** Relatively wide free-fall

**Property Owner:** Pisgah National Forest

**County:** Transylvania

**Trail Rating:** 1, 4 to base

**Trail Length (one-way):** 100-200 yards to the base depending on where you park

**Description:** Looking Glass Falls is a stunningly beautiful waterfall with a large pool at the base. The sheer rock face alongside the falls adds to the breathtaking scenery. Its beauty and ease of access makes this one of the most popular and most photographed waterfalls in the Appalachian Mountains.

It is rare that you will have this waterfall all to yourself, except maybe in winter. It is also common during hot weather to find people swimming and frolicking in the pool below the falls.

**Directions to Trail:** Beginning at the intersection of US 64, US 276, and NC 280 in the town of Pisgah Forest, take US 276 north for approximately 5.5 miles to the paved pullout area on the right.

If you are traveling from the Blue Ridge Parkway take US 276 south for just over 9 miles to the pullout on the left. There are Forest Service signs for the falls coming from either direction to alert you that you are close.

**Trail Directions:** The handicap access observation deck and stairway to the base are at the northern end of the pullout area.

**Photographic Locations:** The falls and rock face can easily be photographed from the observation deck, though you may want to crop out the stairway and handrails. It can be shot from different locations on the stairway but be accommodating to other visitors using the stairs. The base also makes a great location for pictures but you may want to stand back out of reach of the spray from the fall.

# Moore Cove Falls

**Beauty:** 7

**Water Flow:** Small

**Height:** 50 feet

**Type:** Free fall with small cascade at top

**Property Owner:** Pisgah National Forest

**County:** Transylvania

**Trail Rating:** 6

**Trail Length (one-way):** Just over 0.6 mile

**Description:** This is admittedly not the most spectacular waterfall in this region, but what makes it noteworthy is the fascinating cliff face behind the fall. The alternating brown and tan striations in the rock, as well as the sheer size of the cliff face are the most noticeable and pronounced features about this location. It is also attractive due to the ability to walk behind the fall.

The waterfall is named for Adam Moore, a former owner of the property. Another notable previous owner was George W. Vanderbilt, owner of the Biltmore Estate and much of what is now the Pisgah National Forest, who purchased the falls and 50 surrounding acres in 1891 for a paltry $155.

**Directions to Trail:** Beginning at the intersection of US 64, US 276, and NC 280 in the town of Pisgah Forest, take US 276 north for approximately 6.5 miles to the paved pullout area on the right. It is 1 mile north of Looking Glass Falls.

If you are traveling from the Blue Ridge Parkway take US 276 south for just over 8 miles to the pullout on the left. There are Forest Service signs for the falls coming from either direction to alert you that you are close.

**Trail Directions:** The trail begins at the wooden footbridge at the northern end of the pullout. Cross the bridge and follow the trail up the bank. This trail is well maintained and easy to follow. There are wooden footbridges provided when creek crossings are necessary. There are a number of earth and timber steps to negotiate as well. Trail leads directly to the falls.

**Photographic Locations:** Photos can be taken from the trail just before the fall, or just down the bank from the trail on a small clearing in front of the fall. Either of these locations will be good for capturing the entire rock wall. Interesting shots can also be taken from behind the fall.

# Sliding Rock

**Beauty:** 6

**Water Flow:** Small

**Height:** Approximately 30 feet

**Type:** Long smooth cascade

**Property Owner:** Pisgah National Forest

**County:** Transylvania

**Trail Rating:** 1

**Trail Length (one-way):** 100-300 yards depending on where you park

**Description:** Although Sliding Rock is not a true waterfall, I would be doing a great disservice to my readers not to include it. It is an excellent example of a long cascade and a whole lot of fun on a hot summer day. While the beauty rating may only be a 6, the fun rating is definitely a 10. In season you will find this area packed with kids of all ages sliding down the rock face into an 8-foot deep pool of icy water. This is nature's original waterpark and generations of locals and vacationers alike have spent memorable days here. While visiting waterfalls in the area, bring along a swimsuit and give it a try. You will discover why this is one of the region's most popular attractions.

In recent years the Park Service has added restrooms, a bathhouse, observation decks, and walkways. There are lifeguards on duty during tourist season and two large parking areas to accommodate the crowds. A small fee per person is required for admission.

**Directions to Trail:** Beginning at the intersection of US 64, US 276, and NC 280 in the town of Pisgah Forest, take US 276 north for approximately 7.6 miles to the paved parking area on the left. It is just over 1 mile north of Moore Cove Falls.

If you are traveling from the Blue Ridge Parkway take US 276 south for just over 7 miles to the parking area on the right. There are Forest Service signs for the falls coming from either direction to alert you that you are close.

**Trail Directions:** Take the sidewalk at the southern end of the paved parking area to bathhouse, restrooms, decks, and the slide.

**Photographic Locations:** Along the sidewalk beside the slide makes a good location for pictures, as do the observation decks on the side and at the bottom of the slide.

# Waterfall on Cedar Rock Creek

**Beauty:** 7

**Water Flow:** Small

**Height:** 20 feet

**Type:** Short freefalls with small cascades

**Property Owner:** Pisgah National Forest

**County:** Transylvania

**Trail Rating:** 6

**Trail Length (one-way):** 0.8 mile

**Description:** This 20 foot waterfall is composed of short free falls and small cascades in an incredibly beautiful forest setting. Although this fall is relatively small, it is indeed picturesque. It is flanked by moss covered rock walls, as well as a large and very impressive grotto. Combined with native plants and trees around the falls, this is a unique environment well worth the effort to find.

**Directions to Trail:** Beginning at the intersection of US 64, US 276, and NC 280 in the town of Pisgah Forest, take US 276 north for approximately 5.2 miles to F.R. 475 on the left. Follow this road for nearly 1.5 miles to the Pisgah Center for Wildlife Education that is located across the Davidson River on the left. Park in the paved parking lot here.

**Trail Directions:** From the parking area, walk to the bridge blocked by a guardrail, just to the left of the Center, that crosses Cedar Rock Creek. Cross the bridge and take the first trail to the right just past the bridge, Cat Gap Loop Trail. Follow this trail as it parallels the fence. At approximately 0.3 mile there is a wooden footbridge and a gravel road. Cross both and continue on the trail for just over 0.4 mile to a pair of large trees on the left that have fallen over the trail and have been cut away. There will be a rainwater washout just past this point. The trail to the fall begins here on the left and descends down to the falls. If you miss this trail there will be a second one on the left just past a tunnel of mountain laurel. This trail is a bit steeper than the first one but it is shorter. The large grotto will be on your right as you near the fall.

**Photographic Locations:** Great pictures can be taken at a number of locations here. An obvious spot is on the large rocks below the base in front of the falls. Photographs taken from the sides of the fall can be attractive as well, especially when including the moss covered rock walls.

**Beauty:** 7

**Water Flow:** Small

**Height:** 50 feet

**Type:** Numerous cascades and small falls

**Property Owner:** Pisgah National Forest

**County:** Transylvania

**Trail Rating:** 6

**Trail Length (one-way):** 1.25 miles

**Description:** Cove Creek Falls is a collection of cascades and small falls over a rock staircase. It is both impressive and fairly secluded as I was the only one on the trail and at the waterfall. None of the individual falls is very large, but the fact that they collectively cover most of the large rock staircase makes this waterfall a real gem. Not even a considerable amount of downfall at and beyond the base could diminish its appeal.

**Directions to Trail:** Beginning at the intersection of US 64, US 276, and NC 280 in the town of Pisgah Forest, take US 276 north for approximately 5.2 miles to F.R. 475 on the left. Follow this road for nearly 3.2 miles to the paved parking area on the left across from the sign for the Cove Creek Group Camp and the kiosk with a trail map and wildlife information.

**Trail Directions:** Take the gravel road across from the parking area until you reach the Davidson River. At this point go right on the trail, cross the wooden foot bridge and continue to the right on the road. Note the set of cascades on the right halfway to the Caney Bottom Loop Trail which is nearly 0.7 mile from the footbridge. The trail will be on your left just before the group camp, which you can take for 125 yards before turning right where the trail crosses the creek and becomes Cove Creek Trail. You can also reach this trail by cutting across the group camp and picking up the trail running behind it. Take the trail for just under 0.7 mile to a yellow blazed tree on the right marking the trail down to the base. Be careful to stay on Cove Creek Trail and not take Caney Bottom Loop Trail when it turns off.

**Photographic Locations:** There are a couple of locations on the left side that make good spots but the best area for shooting the entire fall is across the pool at the base.

# Jackson Falls
## (Daniel Ridge Falls, Toms Spring Falls)

**Beauty:** 6

**Water Flow:** Small

**Height:** Approximately 100 feet

**Type:** Short falls and cascades

**Property Owner:** Pisgah National Forest

**County:** Transylvania

**Trail Rating:** 3

**Trail Length (one-way):** About 0.5 mile

**Description:** A tall waterfall with small streams that fall and cascade for about 100 feet to a base with piles of boulders. The flow is not terribly impressive but the sheer size of this waterfall is. The surrounding forest also adds to the beauty here.

**Directions to Trail:** Beginning at the intersection of US 64, US 276, and NC 280 in the town of Pisgah Forest, take US 276 north for approximately 5.2 miles to F.R. 475 on the left. Follow this road for just under 4 miles to a gravel parking area and gate on the right just past a single lane concrete bridge over the Davidson River. Park here without blocking the gate.

**Trail Directions:** The trail, which is actually an old logging road, begins at the gate and continues across a new bridge over the Davidson River. The old bridge was destroyed in the floods of 2004 caused by Hurricanes Francis and Ivan. Just north of the river, the trail will fork and you will need to go to the right for almost 0.4 mile to the base of the falls. The Daniel Ridge Loop Trail comes in from the left just before you get to the base.

**Photographic Locations:** To photograph the entire waterfall you may want to shoot from the road, as this is the best location.

# Catheys Creek Falls

**Beauty:** 8

**Water Flow:** Moderate

**Height:** 45 feet

**Type:** Long series of cascades and small falls

**Property Owner:** Pisgah National Forest

**County:** Transylvania

**Trail Rating:** 6

**Trail Length (one-way):** About 100 yards

**Description:** Catheys Creek Falls is a stunningly beautiful steep cascade ending in a shallow pool at the base. Not even large downed trees and other deadfall from previous floods can detract from the outstanding view here. It's waterfalls like this that cause me to run out of adjectives that will adequately describe their beauty.

This waterfall and the creek were named for a Revolutionary War captain, George Cathey, who received land in this area in appreciation for his service to the new nation.

**Directions to Trail:** Beginning at the intersection of US 64, US 276, and NC 280 in the town of Pisgah Forest, take US 276 north for approximately 5.2 miles to F.R. 475 on the left. Follow this road for 6 miles to F.R. 471 (Catheys Creek Road) a gravel road on the left. Take this road for 4.8 miles where there's a small pullout on the left just big enough for a couple of vehicles.

**Trail Directions:** The trail leads downhill from the pullout. It becomes very steep towards the bottom so be careful and grab whatever you can to help you keep your balance.

**Photographic Locations:** There are several good locations around the base to photograph this waterfall. If your balance is good, excellent shots can be taken from a large tree laying across the pool at the base, but be very careful as moisture and algae can make it extremely slippery. There is also a small clearing at the end of the trail that also makes a good location if you're not up for going any farther or balancing on tree trunks.

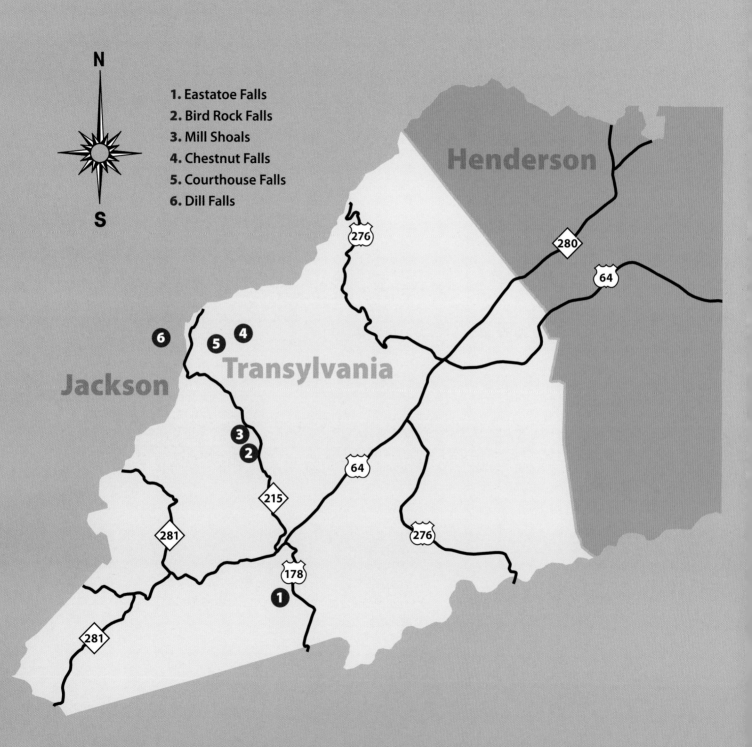

N

S

1. Eastatoe Falls
2. Bird Rock Falls
3. Mill Shoals
4. Chestnut Falls
5. Courthouse Falls
6. Dill Falls

Henderson

Jackson

Transylvania

276

280

64

6

5

4

3

2

215

64

281

276

281

178

1

# CHAPTER 4

# Rosman, Balsam Grove

*Eastatoe Falls*

*Bird Rock Falls*

*Mill Shoals*

*Chestnut Falls*

*Courthouse Falls*

*Dill Falls*

**Beauty:** 8

**Water Flow:** Small

**Height:** 50 feet

**Type:** Short falls and small cascades

**Property Owner:** Private

**County:** Transylvania

**Trail Rating:** 1

**Trail Length (one-way):** About 200 yards

**Description:** A fantastic nearly vertical set of short falls and small cascades dropping to a rock staircase at the bottom. The waterfall is surrounded by trees and native flora, creating an incredible setting and giving the appearance of being much more remote than it actually is. This waterfall would rate very high no matter where it was located.

I was amazed at the freedom of access that was allowed by the property owner, William Dinkins, whom I had the pleasure of meeting on my last visit. Many falls far less attractive have been posted and do not allow public access. It is a truly generous gift to the public to be able to see and experience this stunning waterfall. They maintain the trail and have even installed a set of wooden steps to make access to the base easier and safer. Please act accordingly and be courteous and considerate so that access will continue to be open to everyone.

Mountain Meadows Guest Cabin is available for rent all year. It is a nice, cozy retreat with a fantastic waterfall just across the back yard. For information or to rent it, call (828) 862-3396.

**Directions to Trail:** Beginning at the intersection of US 64 and US 178 just north of Rosman, take US 178 south for 3.5 miles to a small gravel road on the right with a sign for Mountain Meadows Guest Cabin. Take the road next to two ponds and go left at the fork in the driveway in front of the house.

**Trail Directions:** Park in the small gravel lot at the guest cottage to the left of the house. Please do not block the driveway or park in the yard. The trail follows a lane along the wood line on the left side of the back yard and leads to the base of the falls.

**Photographic Locations:** Due to the relatively closed surroundings, the best location is from the area around the base. A vertical shot framed by the bordering greenery makes an excellent picture.

# Bird Rock Falls
## (Birdtown Falls, Cathedral Falls)

**Beauty:** 6

**Water Flow:** Moderate

**Height:** 15 feet

**Type:** Short, wide cascading fall

**Property Owner:** Private

**County:** Transylvania

**Trail Rating:** 4

**Trail Length (one-way):** Approximately 0.25 mile

**Description:** This is a small and fairly unremarkable waterfall when considered by itself. Luckily there is one of the most massive and stunning rock cliffs anywhere in the region as a backdrop. This feature makes this waterfall unique and a must see. This property is owned, and public access is graciously allowed by Living Waters Ministries, so it goes without saying that you should be on your very best behavior when visiting here. On my last visit here, I discovered an empty drink bottle and a dirty diaper, which I promptly removed. This is the kind of irresponsibility that causes private owners of waterfalls to make them off limits to the public. Please show respect and take any trash out with you when you leave.

**Directions to Trail:** From the intersection of US 64 and NC 215, take NC 215 north for 7.6 miles to a pullout on the left side of the road. This point is located just before Living Waters Ministry, also on the left.

If you are traveling south on NC 215 from the Blue Ridge Parkway, Living Waters Ministry will be 9.25 miles south on the right. Just past Living Waters is a pullout on the right.

**Trail Directions:** From the pullout area, there is a short, steep path leading to a T intersection. Take the trail to the left and cross the two footbridges. You will come to another T intersection at an overlook area with a stone fence. Take the left trail. Along the trail are some nice cascades, the short, wide Pleated Rock Falls, and one of the best grottos that you will ever see. It has a fire pit and a stone bench for resting. Just past the grotto, the trail turns right and descends some timber and earth steps and comes out on a wide, sloping rock that can be very slippery when wet. You will obviously know you've reached the falls when you see the huge cliff face.

**Photographic Locations:** The best shots are either from downstream or profiling the falls on the right side, capturing both the falls and the cliff face.

# Mill Shoals
## *(French Broad Falls)*

**Beauty:** 7

**Water Flow:** Large (combined)

**Height:** About 15 feet each

**Type:** One freefall and one staircase fall with a small cascade in-between

**Property Owner:** Private

**County:** Transylvania

**Trail Rating:** 3

**Trail Length (one-way):** Very short

**Description:** This is a unique location actually containing three falls. There is one freefall, one cascading staircase fall, and a third smaller cascade between the two larger falls. They are located directly behind Living Waters Ministries, which is also the owner of the property. Please be careful not to disturb the residents, and show respect and your appreciation for being allowed access to this magnificent place by being on your best behavior while here.

**Directions to Trail:** See directions for Bird Rock Falls.

**Trail Directions:** See trail directions for Bird Rock Falls. Take the trail to the right at the first T intersection to the edge of the river.

**Photographic Locations:** The best location is downstream from the falls either in or along the riverbed, or from large rocks in the middle of the river. From this location you can capture all of the falls, the river, and the rock formations with a good horizontal shot.

# Chestnut Falls

**Beauty:** 6

**Water Flow:** Small

**Height:** 15 feet

**Type:** Sliding cascade

**Property Owner:** Pisgah National Forest

**County:** Transylvania

**Trail Rating:** 4

**Trail Length (one-way):** Just under 1.0 mile

**Description:** A small but very attractive cascading waterfall over a green moss covered rock face. It is located in a beautiful spot along Kiesee Creek surrounded by trees, mountain laurel, and moss covered rocks. It is easy to see why there is a campsite here, as it would be a great place to stay.

**Directions to Trail:** From the intersection of US 64 and NC 215 near Rosman, take NC 215 north for approximately 11 miles to F.R. 140 (Courthouse Creek Road) on the right. Proceed on F.R. 140 for 2.65 miles to a gate on the right. This is Kiesee Creek Road. Park here without blocking the gate.

From the Blue Ridge Parkway, F.R. 140 is 6.5 miles south and is located on the left.

**Trail Directions:** Go around the gate take the grassy Kiesee Creek Road that will gradually ascend and descend. This is a fairly easy old logging road to hike. Continue for just over 0.75 mile to a grassy clearing where the road forks. Just as you reach the clearing, there will be a trail on the left. Take this trail as it winds through the forest. It will lead to a campsite on Kiesee Creek. The falls are just upstream from the campsite. The trail will get you part of the way, you will then have to carefully negotiate the rocks in the creek to get to the falls.

**Photographic Locations:** Just downstream from the falls on the rocks in the creek bed make the best locations for shooting this waterfall. Be careful here as the rocks can be very slippery. Also take care not to disturb the moss covering the rocks.

**Beauty:** 8

**Water Flow:** Small

**Height:** 40 feet

**Type:** Narrow freefall

**Property Owner:** Pisgah National Forest

**County:** Transylvania

**Trail Rating:** 5

**Trail Length (one-way):** .35 mile

**Description:** This breathtakingly beautiful waterfall is unique among the region's falls. It is a diagonal flume flowing into a deep pool in a horseshoe-shaped natural amphitheater created from the surrounding rock face. It makes an inviting swimming hole that many locals and some not-so-locals take advantage of for cooling off on hot summer days.

**Directions to Trail:** From the intersection of US 64 and NC 215 near Rosman, take NC 215 north for approximately 11 miles to F.R. 140 (Courthouse Creek Road) on the right. Proceed on F.R. 140 for 3 miles to a small pullout on the right just past the fourth bridge, which crosses Courthouse Creek. Summey Cove Trail is across the road and follows the creek.

From the Blue Ridge Parkway, F.R. 140 is 6.5 miles south and is located on the left.

**Trail Directions:** Take Summey Cove Trail from F.R. 140 to a trail on the left leading down to the falls. There is a set of steps leading to the base at the end of the trail. Total distance is roughly .35 mile.

**Photographic Locations:** There are several good spots around the edge of the pool at the base. This is a very hard waterfall to photograph due to dramatic lighting differences from one side of the amphitheater to the other if there is sun shining into the area of the falls. As with most waterfalls, the best time to shoot this one is either when it's overcast or when there is some cloud cover.

# Dill Falls

**Beauty Rating:** 7

**Water Flow:** Small

**Height:** 60 feet

**Type:** Short falls with a long cascades

**Property Owner:** Nantahala National Forest

**County:** Jackson

**Trail Difficulty:** 3

**Trail Length (one-way):** 0.75 mile

**Description:** Dill Falls is a tall, narrow cascading fall down an exposed rock face, ending in a small pool at the base. The upper area is a short freefall, while the lower area is a series of cascades and short falls. It is set in a beautiful location along Tanasee Creek with large rocks and some deadfall around the edge of the pool.

**Directions to Trail:** From the intersection of US 64 and NC 215, take NC 215 north for approximately 11 miles to F.R. 4663 on the left. The road goes between two homesites. Proceed for 1.8 miles where you'll come to an area where F.R 4663 turns hard right and F.R. 4663B forks off to the left and descends. Take F.R. 4663B unless your vehicle has low clearance. If so you will need to park nearby and continue on foot. Continue on F.R. 4663B for just over 0.5 mile to a point where three roads branch off. The road straight is overgrown, the center road descends and goes to Dill Falls, and the ascending road to the right goes to Upper Dill Falls. Park here.

**Trail Directions:** Take the center road for almost 0.2 mile to the creek and turn right. You'll be just downstream from the base of the falls.

To reach Upper Dill Falls, take the road to the right from the parking spot and follow the road as it ascends. About 200 yards after the road levels out you will be able to hear the falls down to your left. You will need to locate the faint steep trail down the bank to get to the falls.

**Photographic Locations:** The base area, as with many falls, is the location to shoot this waterfall. From the large rocks in the creek bed or even on a large tree that has fallen across the creek, there are a number of locations to get good shots.

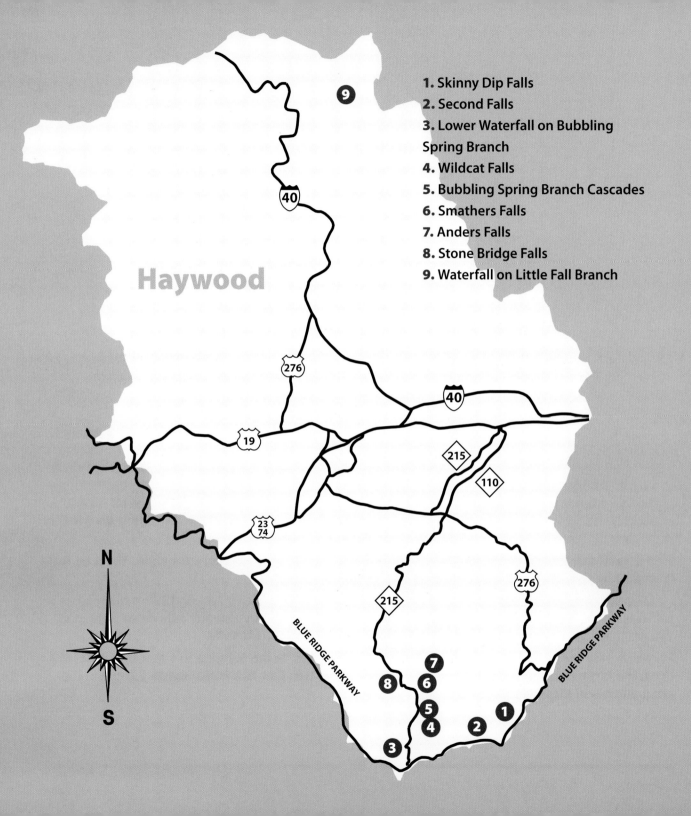

1. **Skinny Dip Falls**
2. **Second Falls**
3. **Lower Waterfall on Bubbling Spring Branch**
4. **Wildcat Falls**
5. **Bubbling Spring Branch Cascades**
6. **Smathers Falls**
7. **Anders Falls**
8. **Stone Bridge Falls**
9. **Waterfall on Little Fall Branch**

Haywood

# CHAPTER 5

# Haywood County

# Skinny Dip Falls

**Beauty:** 7

**Water Flow:** Small

**Height:** 30 feet total

**Type:** Short cascading falls

**Property Owner:** Pisgah National Forest

**County:** Haywood

**Trail Rating:** 5

**Trail Length (one-way):** 0.4 mile

**Description:** Several short cascading falls that descend into an absolutely perfect pool at the base and a further chute under a footbridge at the end of the trail. It is easy to see how this waterfall got its name, although all you are likely to see now are locals and a few lucky travelers in shorts and swimsuits enjoying one of the best natural swimming pools in the region. Combined with gorgeous wilderness surroundings, this spot is truly a gem and well worth a stop to check it out, not to mention a cool dip on a hot summer day.

**Directions to Trail:** If you are traveling on the Blue Ridge Parkway, park at the Looking Glass Rock Overlook located at Milepost 417.

From NC 215, travel north on the Parkway to the overlook. From US 276, take the Parkway to the south. The overlook is located between NC 215 and US 276.

**Trail Directions:** The trail starts across the Parkway from the northern end of the overlook. After several hundred yards you will climb a set of steps and come to an intersection with the Mountains-to-Sea Trail. Continue going straight, which will be the Mountains-to-Sea Trail, for a short and fairly level stretch. The trail then begins to descend over a rocky and root filled section that requires some care to negotiate. The falls will appear ahead after a short distance.

**Photographic Locations:** There is a ledge across the creek from the pool where I took most of my pictures, but be careful not to slide down the incline like I did, as it is very slippery here. The edge of the pool makes a nice location, as does the end of the trail near the footbridge. Almost any picture at this waterfall will be good.

# Second Falls

**Beauty:** 7

**Water Flow:** Small

**Height:** 55 feet

**Type:** Cascading stair step falls

**Property Owner:** Pisgah National Forest

**County:** Haywood

**Trail Rating:** 5

**Trail Length:** 0.3 mile

**Description:** This is an impressive waterfall in any season of the year. It is a wide, cascading fall that stair steps down a large exposed rock formation to a pool and boulder field at the bottom. Framed nicely by trees and foliage on both sides, it is attractive in spring and summer, but most stunning with fall color. This fall is popular with both locals and Parkway travelers looking for a great view, sunbathing spot, or for a quick and cool dip.

**Directions to Trail:** The trailhead is located at the northern end of the Graveyard Fields Overlook between mile markers 418 and 419 on the Blue Ridge Parkway.

**Trail Directions:** Take the stairs next to the trail map in the parking area down to the paved trail. Follow this to a footbridge over the Yellowstone Prong. After crossing the bridge, take the right trail for approximately 400 feet until you come to another fork. Again take the right trail that leads to a set of descending stairs that will take you to the base of the falls.

The loop trail will also lead you to Upper Falls, a narrow sliding drop that is far less impressive than Second Falls. Upper Falls is 1.6 miles from the Overlook parking area. While the waterfall is not very impressive, the scenery along the trail certainly is. The valley here is uniquely devoid of the dense forest and shrubbery that is characteristic of these mountains, a result of a large wildfire that ravaged this area in 1925. The fire also destroyed the windblown and gray moss covered trees that resembled tombstones, giving the area the name it still has, Graveyard Fields.

**Photographic Locations:** You can get great shots of this fall from the edge of the boulder field off the deck at the bottom of the stairs. If you are a bit more adventurous or want more unobstructed views of the fall, then the best shots are to be taken from the large boulders that line the outer edge of the pool at the base of the falls.

# Lower Waterfall on Bubbling Spring Branch

**Beauty:** 6

**Water Flow:** Small

**Height:** 20 feet

**Type:** Steep cascades

**Property Owner:** Pisgah National Forest

**County:** Haywood

**Trail Rating:** 4

**Trail Length (one-way):** 0.28 mile

**Description:** Yes this waterfall is relatively small and may not fall into the spectacular category, but it is framed by the spectacular Middle Prong Wilderness. The surrounding environment is simply outstanding and aside from the trail and a campsite or two, is still relatively pristine. Coming upon this waterfall in this beautiful setting really completes the scene.

**Directions to Trail:** Beginning at the intersection of NC 215 and the Blue Ridge Parkway, take NC 215 north for 0.4 mile to a gravel parking area on the left.

If you are traveling south on NC 215, the gravel parking area is on the right 8.1 miles south of the Sunburst Campground.

**Trail Directions:** The Mountains-to-Sea Trail is just north of the parking area on the same side of the road. Enter the forest here and continue for about 30 yards until the trail turns left. Just past the turn will be the first of several creek crossings. You'll come to a campsite where you'll need to bear left and cross the creek again. Continue on trail until you will cross the creek a third time, and again at just over 50 yards upstream. After the fourth crossing the trail will end at the creek in about 100 yards or so. At this point you will need to follow the creek bed a short distance until the falls appear. Low water flow usually makes these crossings very easy.

If you want to continue to Upper Waterfall on Bubbling Spring Branch, climb the hill to the left of the base and take the trail upstream. The trail will end at the creek a short distance later, where you will need to follow the creek bed upstream until you reach the falls.

**Photographic Locations:** The best location to photograph this waterfall is from several large rocks in the creek bed just below the base. From this location you can capture all of the cascades, the pool at the base, and the native flora that frames both sides of the falls.

# Wildcat Falls

**Beauty:** 6

**Water Flow:** Small

**Height:** 60 feet

**Type:** Steep cascade

**Property Owner:** Pisgah National Forest

**County:** Haywood

**Trail Rating:** 3

**Trail Length (one-way):** Just under 0.7 mile

**Description:** A long cascade flowing over a slick, relatively flat rock face. It is nicely framed along both sides by trees, mountain laurel, and other native flora.

**Directions to Trail:** From the Blue Ridge Parkway, travel north on NC 215 for .85 mile to a small dirt road on the right with an adjoining parking area. There is a sign alongside the road for a campsite that is just down the logging road from the parking area.

If you are traveling south on NC 215, the dirt road will be on the left 17.3 miles from the intersection of US 276 and NC 215.

**Trail Directions:** From the parking area, take the old logging road and turn right at the campsite. It will continue down the hill and cross the creek. Crossing the creek on the rocks will be a breeze with low flow, but if the water level is up you might get your feet wet. Follow the road for a total of just under 0.7 mile until you get to the falls at a one-lane concrete bridge.

If you continue on the logging road for another 1.25 miles you will come to Flat Laurel Creek Cascades. These are a long series of cascades that are beautiful, interesting, and fun to explore. There will be a washout area on your left that doubles as a bank scramble path to get to the cascades. You will hear the flow as you approach the path.

**Photographic Locations:** You will want to shoot this waterfall from the old concrete bridge over the creek at the base.

# Bubbling Spring Branch Cascades

**Beauty:** 7

**Water Flow:** Small

**Height:** Over 50 feet

**Type:** Steep cascade

**Property Owner:** Pisgah National Forest

**County:** Haywood

**Trail Rating:** 1, 7 to base

**Trail Length (one-way):** Roadside, just over 100 yards to base

**Description:** A long series of cascades and short falls down a wide, exposed rock face creek bed ending in a small pool at the bottom. It is an impressive view from a distance or from the creek bed itself, but there is less to see from the bottom.

**Directions to Trail:** The roadside pullout is located on the right 2.0 miles north of the Blue Ridge Parkway.

If you are traveling south on NC 215, the pullout will be on the left 1.3 miles south of the Triple Arch Bridge.

**Trail Directions:** It can be viewed from both the roadside pullout or by taking the steep trail that begins at the guardrail and proceeds about 100 yards to the bottom of the cascades.

There is a trail along the right side of the cascades that leads to a great swimming hole at the top of the cascades, or you can walk up the bedrock along the cascades if you prefer.

**Photographic Locations:** The roadside pullout makes the best location for photographing these cascades. A vertical shot will capture the entire cascade that is visible from this vantage point.

# Smathers Falls
## (Lower Waterfall on Sam Branch)

**Beauty:** 7

**Water Flow:** Small

**Height:** Approximately 40 feet

**Type:** A long series of cascades and short falls

**Property Owner:** Pisgah National Forest

**County:** Haywood

**Trail Rating:** 4

**Trail Length (one-way):** 0.25 mile

**Description:** A long series of short falls and sliding cascades down a rocky, inclining creek bed. The canopy is open along the creek but trees and mountain laurel grow right down to the edge of the creek bed, making this a very picturesque waterfall.

**Directions to Trail:** From the Blue Ridge Parkway, travel north on NC 215 for 4.2 miles to a pullout in a sharp curve on the right side of the road large enough for several vehicles.

If you are traveling south on NC 215, the pullout will be on the left 14 miles from the intersection of US 276 and NC 215.

**Trail Directions:** The trail starts near the south end of the guardrail and climbs steeply up the hill. It turns left and follows an old logging road to the waterfall. To access the base, you will need to cross the creek and pick up the trail that descends steeply to the left.

**Photographic Locations:** The upper portions of the falls can be photographed from the point where the trail crosses the creek. There are also good locations to capture the lower portions from the large rocks in the creek near the base, but care must be used when shooting from these areas.

# Anders Falls
*(Waterfall in Wash Hollow)*

**Beauty:** 6

**Water Flow:** Very small

**Height:** 45

**Type:** Steep cascade and short falls

**Property Owner:** Pisgah National Forest

**County:** Haywood

**Trail Rating:** 6

**Trail Length (one-way):** Just over 0.3 mile

**Description:** A narrow steep cascade down a slick rock face. The surrounding area of natural flora, a shady canopy, and a small, cool mountain stream make this waterfall one of the more impressive small falls in the region. It definitely attests to the fact that persistence pays off with the extra effort to locate it.

**Directions to Trail:** See directions for Smathers Falls.

**Trail Directions:** See Trail Directions for Smathers Falls. Cross Smathers Falls where the trail meets the creek. Be very careful here as a slip can be hazardous. Pick up the trail across the creek and continue for several hundred yards.

**Photographic Locations:** The best location for photographing this waterfall is slightly downstream, allowing you to capture the falls, the stream, and the surrounding plant life with a good vertical shot. It can also be shot from the end of the trail with less incorporation of the surroundings.

# Stone Bridge Falls
## (Waterfall on West Fork Pigeon River)

**Beauty:** 6

**Water Flow:** Small

**Height:** 20 feet

**Type:** Short falls and small cascades with pools

**Property Owner:** Pisgah National Forest

**County:** Haywood

**Trail Rating:** 1

**Trail Length (one-way):** Roadside

**Description:** A short pounding freefall with small cascades and short falls that drop through a series of stair stepping pools carved out of the exposed rock below the main falls. The stark but incredible rock formations along the series of falls, cascades, and pools makes this a truly unique setting for the region. There is also an interesting single arch stone bridge that can be examined from the creek bed area. This waterfall is easy to reach and its attributes are well worth the time to explore them.

**Directions to Trail:** From the Blue Ridge Parkway, travel north on NC 215 for 4.4 miles to a pullout just past the falls on the left side of the road large enough for a couple of vehicles. If this is full, turn around and park in another pullout 0.1 mile south of the bridge on the left.

If you are traveling south on NC 215, the pullout will be on the right 13.8 miles from the intersection of US 276 and NC 215.

**Trail Directions:** Roadside access. If you are the adventurous type, climb over the guardrail to more closely examine all of the falls, cascades, pools, bridge, and interesting rock formations.

**Photographic Locations:** There are several good locations to photograph the unique features of this area. The view from the top of the bridge makes a good spot, as do the numerous places along the creek on the rock formations, shooting both upstream and downstream.

# Waterfall on Little Fall Branch

**Beauty:** 7

**Water Flow:** Very small

**Height:** 40 feet

**Type:** Very steep cascades and short free falls

**Property Owner:** Pisgah National Forest

**County:** Haywood

**Trail Rating:** 3

**Trail Length (one-way):** 0.3 mile

**Description:** This is a small but very impressive waterfall and a perfect example that a fall doesn't have to have a large flow or big size to be great. The green moss covered cliff and rocks, along with the surrounding forest and native flora make this little waterfall a real prize. I could have stayed here for hours listening to the sounds of falling water and the flowing creek. This is a great place to just sit, listen, and enjoy the beauty of this area.

**Directions to Trail:** From I-40, take Exit 7 (Harmon Den) and go north on Cold Springs Creek Road that changes to gravel almost immediately and becomes FR 148. Continue for 3.7 miles, passing an information kiosk, FR 148A, and the Harmon Den parking area along the way. Turn right on FR 3526 at the brown sign for the Harmon Den Horse Camp and the Cool Springs Picnic Area. Take this road for just over 0.3 mile to a gate on the left and park beside the gate or on the side of the road just past it.

**Trail Directions:** Continue up the road to the next gate less than 100 yards farther. Go around the gate and look for the narrow footpath on the left side just past the gate. Take this path. It will wind through the forest and follow the creek to the falls. This is a very easy hike.

**Photographic Locations:** There are a number of good locations downstream that can produce excellent shots. This is a good one for isolated verticals of just the falls or horizontal shots that include the green moss covered rock face and surrounding trees and foliage. Experiment with different locations and angles and have some fun.

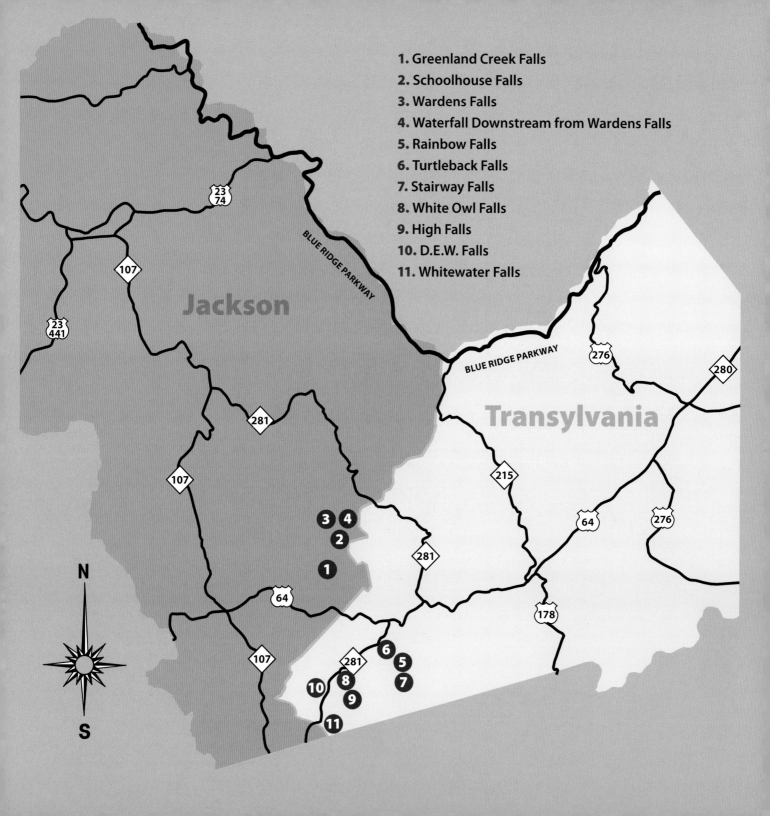

1. Greenland Creek Falls
2. Schoolhouse Falls
3. Wardens Falls
4. Waterfall Downstream from Wardens Falls
5. Rainbow Falls
6. Turtleback Falls
7. Stairway Falls
8. White Owl Falls
9. High Falls
10. D.E.W. Falls
11. Whitewater Falls

# CHAPTER 6

# Panthertown Valley, Sapphire

# Greenland Creek Falls

**Beauty:** 7

**Water Flow:** Small

**Height:** 45 feet

**Type:** Steep cascades with short falls

**Property Owner:** Nantahala National Forest

**County:** Jackson

**Trail Rating:** 4

**Trail Length (one-way):** 1 mile

**Description:** This waterfall actually has two parts, a long steep cascade with a short overhanging fall at the bottom, and a short cascade with a small overhanging drop into a large tea-colored pool. The falls drop down a bold, rounded rock face bordered by trees and shrubs, creating a breathtaking scene. The color of the water is characteristic of many streams in Panthertown Valley and is caused by the presence of tannic acid from the soil and decaying plant matter. Many rivers in eastern North Carolina also have this color, and while it does give the water a different appearance than most mountains streams, it is harmless.

**Directions to Trail:** At the intersection of US 64 and NC 281 east of Lake Toxaway, take NC 281 north for 0.8 mile and turn left on Cold Mountain Road just past the Lake Toxaway Fire Dept. Continue on this road for about 5.5 miles, it turns to an adhered gravel surface at 2.5 miles. The road turns left at a retreat called Canaan Land, where a sign points left for access to Panthertown Valley. After turning left, take the first right and park in a small pullout on the left where the road widens about 100 feet from Cold Mountain Rd.

**Trail Directions:** The trail begins at the pullout and descends gradually before joining an old logging road. Continue on this road for about 0.7 mile to a clearing with a fire ring, cross the clearing and pick up the trail on the other side. Keep straight through a second campsite. Here the trail takes on a different look, narrowing and passing through a tunnel of mountain laurel and rhododendron. The trail meanders around and crosses the creek several times before coming out at the falls.

**Photographic Locations:** There are several good spots around the edge of the pool on large rocks to get great shots. Try shooting from both sides and directly in front to get different looks. Be careful crossing the creek on the rocks.

# Schoolhouse Falls

**Beauty:** 8

**Water Flow:** Moderate

**Height:** 20 feet

**Type:** Short cascade with an overhanging drop

**Property Owner:** Nantahala National Forest

**County:** Jackson

**Trail Rating:** 4, 6 if you take the shorter trail

**Trail Length (one-way):** 1.2 miles

**Description:** This is a picture-perfect waterfall in a stunningly beautiful setting. The top is a short cascade with an overhanging free fall that you can walk behind if you are adventurous enough to cross the pool. It also makes a great swimming hole if you've worked up a lather on the hike, as I can attest from my first visit here. This is about as good as it gets for a relatively short waterfall, and in my opinion, is well deserving of the beauty rating.

**Directions to Trail:** See directions for Greenland Creek Falls. Continue to the end of the short gravel road off of Cold Mountain Rd. where there is a Forest Service gate.

**Trail Directions:** The trail begins to the right of the gate and joins the old access road just across a footbridge over a small creek. Turn left on the road (going right leads to Canaan Land and is private property) and continue for just over 0.5 mile to a trail on the left. Here you have a choice - you can take the shorter but more difficult trail or continue the easier hike on the road. If you take the road, continue until you come to a short brown radio tower where there's a shortcut trail that goes straight off the road in a sharp curve. You can take this trail that rejoins the road later or just continue on the road. You will eventually come to a road bearing right that leads to Wardens Falls, a trail that goes left at 4 roped posts, and a trail on the left just past a foot bridge over the creek. Either trail left will take you to the falls, but the second one is an easier hike.

**Photographic Locations:** Anywhere around the edge of the pool makes a great location to photograph this waterfall, as there are no bad locations.

# Wardens Falls

**Beauty:** 7

**Water Flow:** Moderate

**Height:** 35 feet

**Type:** Long, curving cascades with a small pool

**Property Owner:** Nantahala National Forest

**County:** Jackson

**Trail Rating:** 5, 8 to base

**Trail Length (one-way):** 1.7 miles

**Description:** This is a very interesting and different cascading waterfall. It curves and slides steeply to the right into a small pool before continuing down the smooth rock slope to the base. The pool makes a nice spot to cool off and the lower cascade makes a fun waterslide down to the creek. There were several college students doing just that on my visit.

**Directions to Trail:** See directions for Schoolhouse Falls. Take the road to the right from the intersection with the trails leading to Schoolhouse Falls.

**Trail Directions:** From the intersection, the road will ascend gradually. Follow it for about 0.25 mile until you see a trail on the left as the road turns sharply right. Take this trail for 0.2 mile, passing an area under the power line where there are many fallen trees, to a small clearing. From this clearing, take the small trail to the left that leads to the top of the falls. The path to the right goes to the Waterfall Downstream from Wardens Falls. The left trail descends for just over 0.1 mile to the top of the falls, but just before the falls, there is a trail to the right that goes to the base. It is fairly closed in and a bit of a tight fit and is very steep and slippery as you near the bottom. You will need to hold onto the limbs there to keep from falling down the slope. Proceed slowly and carefully. To get a clear view of the falls you will need to cross the creek as best you can across the rocks there.

**Photographic Locations:** The falls can be photographed from the bottom but the best location is from the ledge opposite the base. Be careful if you decide to shoot from this location as it is often slick.

# Waterfall Downstream from Wardens Falls
## *(Jawbone Falls)*

**Beauty:** 6

**Water Flow:** Moderate

**Height:** About 30 feet

**Type:** Long cascade with small drops

**Property Owner:** Nantahala National Forest

**County:** Jackson

**Trail Rating:** 5

**Trail Length (one-way):** 2.2 miles

**Description:** I will admit that this cascading fall is not the most impressive, but when considered with the surrounding scenery and the large shallow pool, the entire scene is quite a nice find. In spring and early summer there will be blooming shrubbery along both sides of the falls, adding to the attractiveness of this area. In the fall, the color reflecting off the pool is stunning.

**Directions to Trail:** See directions for Wardens Falls.

**Trail Directions:** From the small clearing near Wardens Falls, take the trail to the right. It will ascend for some distance until you come to a creek crossing at about 0.25 mile. At about 0.4 mile you will come to a fork in the trail. The left trail goes to the falls and the right trail leads up to Devils Elbow. Follow the trail to the left until you either see a trail going left or you get to Riding Ford Falls (which is a short wide cascade). The trail to the left just before Riding Ford will lead down to a campsite that you will cross to reach the pool across from the base of the waterfall. If you miss it and arrive at Riding Ford, just turn left at the water and walk a few yards to the clear trail. Take the trail into the woods and across the campsite to the pool.

**Photographic Locations:** The falls can be photographed from the end of the trail at the pool or out along the rocky island. The best shots will include the surrounding flora and the reflections in the large pool.

# Rainbow Falls

**Beauty:** 10

**Water Flow:** Moderate

**Height:** 125 feet

**Type:** A series of broken falls and cascades

**Property Owner:** Nantahala National Forest

**County:** Transylvania

**Trail Rating:** 8

**Trail Length (one-way):** 1.5 miles

**Description:** A tall series of multiple drops and short cascades over a massive exposed rock face. The name comes from rainbows that appear in sunlight from the spray off the falls. Likewise, moonbows are also formed in bright moonlight, though few people see this waterfall at night. In many ways, this is truly a spectacular waterfall.

**Directions to Trail:** Okay, there are some big changes to access Rainbow, Turtleback, and Stairway Falls. Access is no longer available on the old dirt road on NC 281 because it has been closed by the NC Forest Service. You can now use the new, longer, and more difficult trail at the Grassy Ridge Access Area in Gorges State Park on NC 281. Take NC 281 south from US 64 for 0.9 mile to the new entrance on the left. Take the paved road for 1.6 miles to the parking area for the Grassy Ridge Trailhead.

**Trail Directions:** The trail begins at the lower end of the parking area where there is a picnic table along with information and map kiosks. The first mile of the wide new gravel trail is in Gorges State Park. It follows a mostly gradual descent to a T intersection. Take the trail to the right. The gravel will end where you enter the Nantahala National Forest, and you will notice that the trail is not as well maintained. You will cross 2 creeks and come to a large campsite. Keep straight and pick up the trail on the other side. The trail soon begins to narrow and ascend, sometimes sharply, especially as you near the falls. There are a number of side trails that allow you to explore the river along the way. The trail will pass Rainbow Falls along a rail fence.

**Photographic Locations:** The viewing area along the main trail is the best location to shoot this fall. You can isolate the fall with a vertical shot or capture the fall, rock formation, pool, and surrounding vegetation with a horizontal shot. The wildflowers along the rail fence make a great foreground. There is also a lower observation area to get closer shots. Just past the rail fence a side trail to the left descends to this area.

# Turtleback Falls

**Beauty:** 7

**Water Flow:** Moderate

**Height:** 10 feet

**Type:** Upper rounded cascade with short overhanging falls

**Property Owner:** Nantahala National Forest

**County:** Transylvania

**Trail Rating:** 8

**Trail Length (one-way):** Just over 1.5 miles

**Description:** A short wide waterfall with a rounded upper cascade that drops over a staggered overhang. Falls drop into a deep pool that has long been a popular swimming spot for locals, as evidenced by a rope on the left side for climbing up after sliding down the cascade. It is certainly understandable that this would be a popular spot, as the slide and pool look very inviting.

**Directions to Trail:** See directions for Rainbow Falls.

**Trail Directions:** Continue on the trail upstream from Rainbow Falls for about 200 yards. It will pass the above the pool at the base of the falls and continue across a footbridge for access along the right side.

**Photographic Locations:** The large rock at the edge of the pool across from the fall makes the best location for pictures. A horizontal shot here will capture the stream, falls, pool, surrounding forest, and anyone taking the plunge.

# Stairway Falls
## *(Keystone Falls, Staircase Falls, Stairstep Falls)*

**Beauty:** 7

**Water Flow:** Moderate

**Height:** 50 feet

**Type:** Long stairstep cascade

**Property Owner:** Nantahala National Forest

**County:** Transylvania

**Trail Rating:** 7

**Trail Length (one-way):** 1.35 miles

**Description:** A long cascade that flows over descending rock ledges, resembling a stairway, with short drops at the base. It is a no-brainer as to how this waterfall got its name. A large pool and lush forest complete a very attractive scene.

**Directions to Trail:** See directions for Rainbow Falls.

**Trail Directions:** See trail directions for Rainbow Falls. From the large campsite just inside the Nantahala National Forest on the trail to Rainbow Falls, take the trail to the left that leads to the river and another campsite. Downstream there are 2 trails leaving the campsite. Take the one on the left that goes into the forest. Follow it on a fairly level grade to a creek crossing and pick up the trail on the other side. Continue on the trail as it weaves through the forest. There will be some deadfall, rocks, and roots to negotiate as the trail ascends and descends as you get nearer to the falls. There are side trails that lead to the river along the way that allow you to explore the upper "steps." The trail will end at the river just downstream from the pool.

**Photographic Locations:** The large rocks just downstream from the pool make the best location for shooting the entire waterfall including the small drops at the top. A horizontal shot here will also capture the pool and surrounding forest.

# White Owl Falls

**Beauty:** 7

**Water Flow:** Moderate

**Height:** 15 feet

**Type:** Multiple cascades and short falls

**Property Owner:** Nantahala National Forest

**County:** Transylvania

**Trail Rating:** 4

**Trail Length (one-way):** 0.17 mile

**Description:** This is one of the more different and remarkable waterfalls in the region, although certainly not the largest. The numerous individual cascades and falls flow over and incredible vertically layered rock formation that has distinctly different looks from the top and the base. The flows drop into a large pool at the base. The setting has a remote feeling despite its closeness to the highway and is nicely closed in by the surrounding forest. Overall, this is quite a beautiful and interesting waterfall.

White Owl Falls makes a quick but rewarding short side trip if you are going to Whitewater Falls or accessing the falls along the Horsepasture or Thompson Rivers.

**Directions to Trail:** Beginning at the intersection of US 64 and NC 281, take NC 281 south for 3.7 miles to Brewer Rd. (SR 1189) on your left. Park along the wide shoulder on the right side of Brewer Rd.

**Trail Directions:** Walk south down NC 281 to the beginning of the second guardrail. The trail begins there near an old concrete drainage spillway. Follow the trail down through the rocks to the top of the falls. It will continue to the left to the creek below the base and pool.

**Photographic Locations:** Anywhere from the rocks in the creek bed makes an excellent location for pictures of this fall. Either side of the creek below the pool also make good spots.

# High Falls

**Beauty:** 8

**Water Flow:** Moderate

**Height:** 55 feet

**Type:** Steep sliding cascade

**Property Owner:** Nantahala National Forest

**County:** Transylvania

**Trail Rating:** 7

**Trail Length (one-way):** 1.4 miles

**Description:** This is a fairly isolated waterfall and is an outstanding example of a steep sliding cascade. The river flows over a wide exposed rock face into an attractive pool that makes a great spot for cooling off. It is set in beautiful surroundings and quickly became one of my favorites.

**Directions to Trail:** See directions for White Owl Falls.

**Trail Directions:** The trail begins at an old gravel logging road located at the junction of NC 281 and Brewer Rd. The road ascends gradually to a yellow gate and the trail goes around it on the right. Continue on the logging road, avoiding several side trails. At just under 1 mile, as the trail begins to descend noticeably, there will be a red clay trail branching to the right. Take this trail. It will ascend gradually and follow the ridge around to the right. You will notice at this point that you are actually on another logging road. Follow this road for a total of 0.4 mile to a small trail to the left. It is marked by a small pile of rocks and pink and orange ribbons tied to trees. Take this trail as it zigzags and descends to the river. The trail is well marked by ribbons to follow. Once at the river, the trail turns right and follows the river to the falls. There will be a small stream with slippery rocks to cross and some deadfall and other limbs and roots to negotiate. This is the part of the trail that rates a 7. The trail comes out on the river just downstream from the pool and the falls.

**Photographic Locations:** This waterfall is tough to shoot if you don't like to get wet. You can't photograph it from the end of the trail. The best locations for shooting it are from in the pool or from boulders across the pool. Both locations will require you to get wet but that shouldn't discourage you. Simply plan for this contingency and enjoy the experience.

# D.E.W. Falls

**Beauty:** 6

**Water Flow:** Small

**Height:** 10-15 feet

**Type:** Sloping cascades with a short free fall

**Property Owner:** Nantahala National Forest

**County:** Transylvania

**Trail Rating:** 4

**Trail Length (one-way):** Just under 200 yards

**Description:** This is a short waterfall with sloping upper cascades and a short free fall. It is a relatively small waterfall but it's easy to get to and is in a picture perfect setting. What it lacks in size, it more than makes up for in beauty.

The unusual name is incredibly significant. It is named for Dorothy Ehrlich Walker, a student at the Hammond School in Columbia, SC. She was killed in an automobile accident in the summer before her senior year at the school. Her classmates cleared the trail to the falls and named it in her honor. Whether or not you think this waterfall is great, the story of its naming certainly is. Kudos to those students whose thoughtful and selfless gifts continue to benefit all who visit here.

**Directions to Trail:** Beginning at the intersection of US 64 and NC 281, take NC 281 south for 5.0 miles to a gravel road on the right. This is the entrance to a campsite with a picnic table and a gate. Park here without blocking the gate.

**Trail Directions:** Go around the gate and take the road to the right that ascends the hill. After less than 100 yards there will be a blue blazed trail on the left that winds down through the forest. After less than 100 yards on the trail, you will come out at the shallow pool just across from the falls.

**Photographic Locations:** The best location for shooting this fall is directly across the shallow pool at the end of the trail. The reflection of the falls on the water adds nicely to the beautiful setting.

# Whitewater Falls

**Beauty:** 10

**Water Flow:** Moderate

**Height:** Over 400 feet

**Type:** Multi-layered drops and cascades

**Property Owner:** Nantahala National Forest

**County:** Transylvania

**Trail Rating:** 3, 6 to observation deck

**Trail Length (one-way):** 0.25 mile to observation deck (sign at start of trail incorrectly says 0.5 mile)

**Description:** One look will clearly show why this is the most popular and arguably the most spectacular waterfall in all of the eastern U.S. It easily deserves a rating of 10. It is one of the most recognizable and most photographed waterfalls anywhere in the country. You cannot help but be in awe of its amazing size and beauty.

This is now a fee area and there is a drop box at the kiosk for paying on the honor system. Before you start laughing, the fee is small and the vast majority of the proceeds go towards maintenance and improvements for guest facilities, so we all benefit.

**Directions to Trail:** At the intersection of US 64 and NC 281, take NC 281 south for just under 9 miles to a paved parking lot on the left. There is a Forest Service sign on the right pointing the way into the parking area.

**Trail Directions:** Paved trail starts at the information kiosk next to the parking lot and continues up a gradual ascent to the upper overlook.

**Photographic Locations:** You can either shoot the falls from the end of the paved trail at a rail fence or from the better location on the observation deck at the base of the stairs.

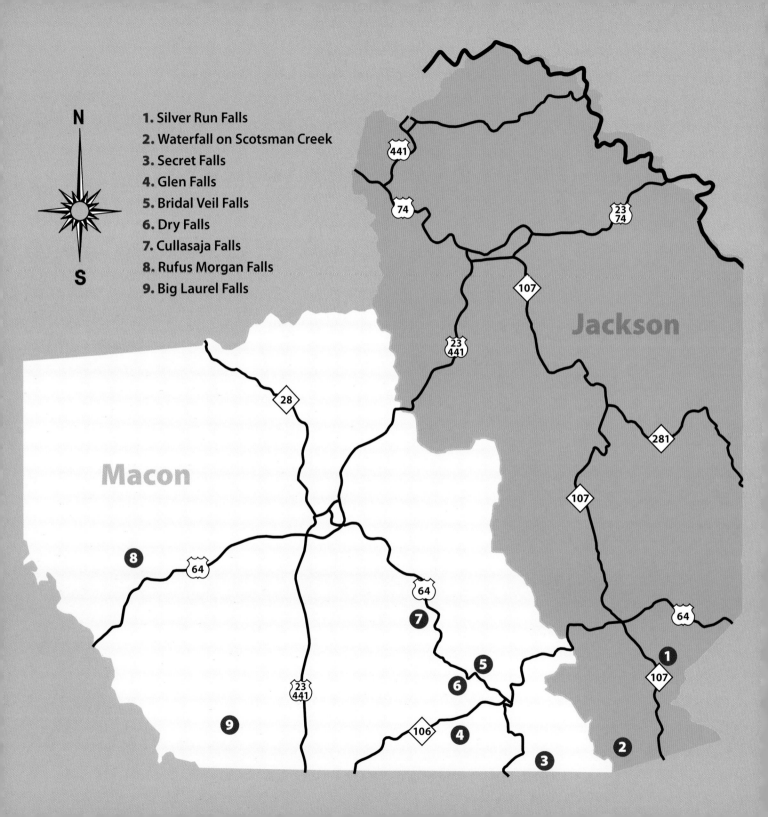

N

S

1. Silver Run Falls
2. Waterfall on Scotsman Creek
3. Secret Falls
4. Glen Falls
5. Bridal Veil Falls
6. Dry Falls
7. Cullasaja Falls
8. Rufus Morgan Falls
9. Big Laurel Falls

Jackson

Macon

# CHAPTER 7

# Cashiers, Highlands, Franklin

*Silver Run Falls*

*Waterfall on Scotsman Creek*

*Secret Falls*

*Glen Falls*

*Bridal Veil Falls*

*Dry Falls*

*Cullasaja Falls*

*Rufus Morgan Falls*

*Big Laurel Falls*

# Silver Run Falls

**Beauty:** 7

**Water Flow:** Small

**Height:** 30 feet

**Type:** Short falls and sliding cascades

**Property Owner:** Nantahala National Forest

**County:** Jackson

**Trail Rating:** 2

**Trail Length (one-way):** Just over 200 yards

**Description:** This waterfall consists of two narrow falls that start as short cascades, then continue as short free falls, and end as steep cascades flowing into a large pool. The pool is absolutely gorgeous, surrounded by trees and shrubs, and containing some interesting rocks. I challenge anyone to find a more beautiful waterfall pool anywhere. Though there were no swimmers during my visit, it should be a local hot spot for cooling off during the summer. Give it a try on your visit.

**Directions to Trail:** From the intersection of US 64 and NC 107 in downtown Cashiers, travel south on NC 107 for 4.0 miles to a pullout on the left. There is a National Forest sign at the pullout.

**Trail Directions:** Gravel trail begins at the pullout and continues through the forest and over a footbridge. It comes out at the pool or you can continue for several yards around the pool to reach the left side of the base.

**Photographic Locations:** The large rocks at the edge of the pool make an excellent location for photographs. Another good location for profile shots is from the large rocks on the left side of the falls. A great location for shooting "we were here" pictures is from the left side of the falls with the subject(s) on the large rock to the left of the base.

# Waterfall on Scotsman Creek

**Beauty:** 7

**Water Flow:** Small

**Height:** 50 feet

**Type:** Overhanging freefalls with lower cascades

**Property Owner:** Nantahala National Forest

**County:** Jackson

**Trail Rating:** 9

**Trail Length (one-way):** About 0.25 mile from gated road

**Description:** This is a remarkable waterfall with several overhanging freefalls that drop onto boulders and a large exposed rock shelf before cascading over and around some interesting rock formations. These have been carved out by cascading water over centuries. You will likely have this waterfall all to yourself due to the difficult trail and the remoteness of the location. If you like a challenge when waterfall hunting, this is one for you.

**Directions to Trail:** From the intersection of US 64 and NC 107 in downtown Cashiers, travel south on NC 107 for 7.0 miles to a right on Bull Pen Road (SR 1100). This is 3.0 miles south of the pullout for Silver Run Falls. Take Bull Pen Road for 4.2 miles to the nearly hidden and gated FR 4564 on the right. Park here. Bull Pen Road turns to gravel at 3.1 miles and FR 4564 will be 0.6 mile past a campsite on the left and McCall Road on the right.

**Trail Directions:** The faint trail begins just after the next right turn, so walk up the road and around the sharp right curve. The trail is not very pronounced and is steep as it winds down through the forest and considerable deadfall. You will be able to hear the falls from the curve so it will help guide you to the base. The lower portion of the trail is very steep and slippery and you will need to hold onto whatever you can get a grip on to help you maintain your balance climbing down and back up. This descent and ascent back up are not for the faint of heart.

**Photographic Locations:** There are a number of good locations to photograph this waterfall. Among them are anywhere along the rock shelf in front of the falls, the end of the trail, and from the exposed rock formations at the bottom. To get a shot excluding the sky you will need to shoot from either the right or left of the falls on the rock shelf. The wet rocks are extremely slippery so be very careful here.

# Secret Falls

**Beauty:** 7

**Water Flow:** Small

**Height:** 40 feet

**Type:** Short falls and cascades

**Property Owner:** Nantahala National Forest

**County:** Macon

**Trail Rating:** 7

**Trail Length (one-way):** 0.66 mile

**Description:** This is a beautiful and unusual waterfall consisting of upper falls and cascades that funnel down to a chute at the bottom. There is also a smaller fall just downstream from the pool. While this might have been a well-kept secret in the past, hence the name, the trail will let you know that it is not the secret that it used to be. You are still likely to have this waterfall all to yourself, however, especially if there are no other cars parked in the clearing at the trailhead.

**Directions to Trail:** From downtown Highlands, take Horse Cove Road (Main St.) east for 3.8 miles and turn right on Walking Stick Road (S.R. 1608). Take Walking Stick Road. for nearly 3 miles to a right turn on F.R. 4567. You will cross a one-lane bridge and a branch over a low concrete culvert along Walking Stick Rd. Stay on F.R. 4567 for 0.25 mile to a grassy clearing on the left. Park here.

The gate at F.R. 4567 is closed from December 15 through March 15. If you visit during this period, park at the gate and add 0.25 mile to the hiking distance.

**Trail Directions:** Big Shoals Trail follows an old logging road at the right rear of the clearing. Continue on the trail as it leaves and rejoins the logging road, though you may not notice the changes. You will cross two streams and begin a gradual ascent, which will level out. At this point look for a trail on the left that descends. Take this trail and negotiate the downfall to a campsite in a clearing. Pick up the trail again on the right after you walk through the clearing. It will become narrow and steep as it winds down to the pool below the base of the falls.

**Photographic Locations:** This waterfall can be well photographed from the end of the trail or from rocks around the left side of the pool.

# Glen Falls
## *(Glenn Falls)*

**Beauty:** 7

**Water Flow:** Small

**Height:** Over 600 feet total

**Type:** Long and short falls with numerous cascades

**Property Owner:** Nantahala National Forest

**County:** Macon

**Trail Rating:** 6

**Trail Length (one-way):** 0.7 mile to base

**Description:** A very long series of cascades and falls stretching for hundreds of feet. Upper cascades can be viewed from a couple of overlooks on side trails. Overlooks have handrails for your safety, as the wet rocks are extremely slippery. In addition to cascades at the overlooks, you can see some very interesting light striations in the rock formations.

The main section of falls consists of several individual falls and cascades over an impressive large exposed rock face leading to another series of cascades and more sections of falls.

**Directions to Trail:** From the intersection of US 64 and NC 106 in Highlands, take NC 106 south for 1.8 miles to a left on Holt Road. There is a Forest Service sign on the right alerting you to the turn. Just as you make the left onto Holt Road, make an immediate right onto Glen Falls Road (S.R. 1618). Take Glen Falls Road for 1.1 miles to a gravel loop with room to park.

**Trail Directions:** The trail begins at the kiosk and bears left. The Chinquapin Mountain Trail starts just after the kiosk and goes to the right, but stay straight. The trail will descend fairly steeply and you will need to negotiate constructed steps as well as natural steps of roots and rocks. Side trails lead to various overlooks at the upper cascades, the top and base of the main section of falls, as well as the bases of the second and third sets of falls. Below this point the limited views and difficult access do not warrant the effort of going any farther.

**Photographic Locations:** Best locations are from the bases of the two main sections of falls, and from the overlook at the top of the first fall, where you can get some excellent shots of the mountain landscape. Stay behind the railings here. A number of people didn't and ended up falling over the edge and sustaining serious injuries.

# Bridal Veil Falls

**Beauty:** 5

**Water Flow:** Very small

**Height:** 60 feet

**Type:** Upper cascade and overhanging fall

**Property Owner:** Nantahala National Forest

**County:** Macon

**Trail Rating:** 1

**Trail Length (one-way):** Roadside

**Description:** An upper cascade with a thin, narrow overhanging free fall, not in itself an outstanding description, but what sets this fall apart is that you can actually drive behind it. Good luck finding another one with that characteristic. It is well worth the few minutes it will take you to stop and take pictures, or the few seconds it will take to drive through. And just imagine being able to tell your friends, family, or co-workers that you drove behind a waterfall on your vacation.

**Directions to Trail:** Bridal Veil Falls is located on US 64 0.45 mile west of the Highlands City Limit and 0.8 mile east of Dry Falls.

**Trail Directions:** Roadside view or drive through. How about that for a different set of trail directions?

**Photographic Locations:** Entire fall with upper cascade can be photographed with a vertical shot from across the road on the other side of the guardrail. Closer shots of the free fall and overhang can be shot from either end of the paved pullout.

# Dry Falls

**Beauty:** 8

**Water Flow:** Moderate

**Height:** 65 feet

**Type:** Long falls with lower cascades

**Property Owner:** Nantahala National Forest

**County:** Macon

**Trail Rating:** 3

**Trail Length (one-way):** About 200 yards

**Description:** A spectacular waterfall with long falls and cascades at the bottom. Those are great characteristics for any waterfall but you can walk behind this one with plenty of room to spare. Although it's called Dry Falls, don't count on staying dry if you decide to walk behind it. There is a generous amount of spray coming off the curtain.

Dry falls was closed for about two years for construction of a new parking area and a handicapped accessible observation deck to make viewing the falls possible for persons with limited mobility. The renovations are completed and the results are fantastic compared with the previous facilities. There are future plans to refurbish the trail down to the falls.

**Directions to Trail:** Dry Falls is located along US 64 almost 5 miles east of Cullasaja Falls and 1.25 miles west of the Highlands City Limit. There are Forest Service signs alerting you to the parking area from both directions.

**Trail Directions:** The trail is easy to find and follow. It starts at the western end of the parking area and winds down steps and damp walkways that are sometimes downright wet. Walk carefully in wet areas, especially on steps as it can get slick. Winter brings new hazards, as these areas will freeze, so proceed with caution.

**Photographic Locations:** Along the walkway on either side of the falls will yield excellent pictures, including people walking behind the water curtain. Shots from behind the falls can produce some unique photos that you won't be able to get at any other waterfall in the state.

# Cullasaja Falls

**Beauty:** 10

**Water Flow:** Moderate

**Height:** About 200 feet

**Type:** Long cascades with numerous falls

**Property Owner:** Nantahala National Forest

**County:** Macon

**Trail Rating:** 1

**Trail Length (one-way):** Roadside

**Description:** Wow! What a magnificent sight this waterfall is. Its upper falls and cascades snake back and forth, feeding numerous finger-like falls that pound out an impressive roar that is clearly audible from the highway. This is one of those rare waterfalls that makes enthusiasts drool and causes even non-enthusiasts to stop and look in awe. It is a shame that it is located where there isn't better access.

One can only imagine the reactions of members of Hernando DeSoto's expeditionary force that traveled through here in 1540. Credited with being the first explorers to this area, the Spanish commander DeSoto and his army would likely have been the first Europeans to see it.

**Directions to Trail:** Falls are located on US 64 west of Highlands. If you are traveling west on US 64, falls will be on the left in a curve 0.45 mile west of Jackson Hole Gem Mining. There is a pullout on the left but it is dangerous to cross the road here. Continue west to a safe location to turn around and come back.

If you are traveling east on US 64 towards Highlands, the pullout for the falls will be on the right, 0.45 mile past the Forest Service sign for the Cullasaja River Gorge.

**Trail Directions:** Roadside viewing. There is a very steep trail across the guardrail that leads to the area near the base. The view from the base isn't nearly as good as the roadside view so you might want to save your energy for exploring more falls.

**Photographic Locations:** The best location for getting great pictures of this waterfall is just over the guardrail in the curve. You will see a worn area where others have been. It is also much safer here as the road is narrow and curvy along this stretch and traffic will be coming out of a blind curve.

# Rufus Morgan Falls

**Beauty:** 7

**Water Flow:** Small

**Height:** 60 feet

**Type:** Long sliding cascade

**Property Owner:** Nantahala National Forest

**County:** Macon

**Trail Rating:** 5

**Trail Length (one-way):** 0.5 mile

**Description:** This steep, sliding cascade is set in a nearly enclosed canopy of beautiful mountain forest. Not only does this fall have the appearance of being in the remote wilderness, it actually is, at least as remote as is fairly easily accessible anyway.

This waterfall is a fitting tribute to Albert Rufus Morgan, an ardent conservationist, poet, and Episcopal priest who was a pioneer in helping to create the Appalachian Trail and is credited with single-handedly maintaining a 50-mile section.

**Directions to Trail:** From Franklin, take US 64 west past the US 64 & US 441/23 interchange just under 4 miles to a right at Old Murphy Road. The Mount Hope Baptist Church will be on the left. Take Old Murphy Road. for 0.1 mile to a left on Wayah Road. Continue on Wayah Road. for 6.45 miles, passing the LBJ Job Corps Civilian Conservation Center, to a gravel road, F.R. 388, on the left. Follow this road for just over 2 miles to a small parking area on the right with a sign for the trailhead.

**Trail Directions:** Trail begins at the parking area and ascends steadily. You will cross a small branch and then a creek on a small footbridge. Both are easy. You will pass an intersection with a crossing trail but keep straight. You will come to a smaller cascade just below the falls and then to a fork in the trail. Take the sharp right to reach the base.

**Photographic Locations:** The area around the base provides the only area to get a good photo of the entire cascade with a vertical shot. You can shoot farther back but there is a tree and a large rock to contend with.

# Big Laurel Falls

**Beauty:** 8

**Water Flow:** Small

**Height:** 20 feet

**Type:** Short upper falls with lower cascades and falls

**Property Owner:** Nantahala National Forest

**County:** Macon

**Trail Rating:** 3

**Trail Length (one-way):** 0.55 mile

**Description:** Wow! What a gorgeous waterfall. There are short twin upper falls with lower cascades and small falls that flow into a fantastic pool.

It may be relatively small but what it lacks in size it more than makes up for in beauty. It instantly became one of my favorites. The breathtaking surroundings really complete the scene. I found it to be one of the most picturesque waterfalls I've ever seen. The rocks and trees around the falls and pool are covered with green moss, as they are on most of the trail.

**Directions to Trail:** From Franklin, take US 64 west 12 miles past the interchange of US 64 and US 441/23 to Old Murphy Road on the left. There will be a sign for Standing Indian Campground. Take Old Murphy Road for 2.0 miles to a right on F.R. 67, where there is a forest service sign for the campground. Continue on F.R. 67 to a fork at 1.78 miles. The right fork goes to the campground, take the left fork for 5.1 miles to the trailhead on the right. Park here.

**Trail Directions:** The trail starts at the trailhead sign and descends to a junction where you need to go right. It continues to a footbridge across the creek and to another junction where you will again go to the right. You will go through a very wet section lined with timbers and roots and into a near tunnel of mountain laurel. This hike is reminiscent of a rain forest due to the moisture and the moss covering nearly every rock and tree. You may also notice that the creeks change if you pay close attention. The trail ends just downstream from the pool at the base.

**Photographic Locations:** The best location to shoot this waterfall is from the rocks just downstream from the pool.

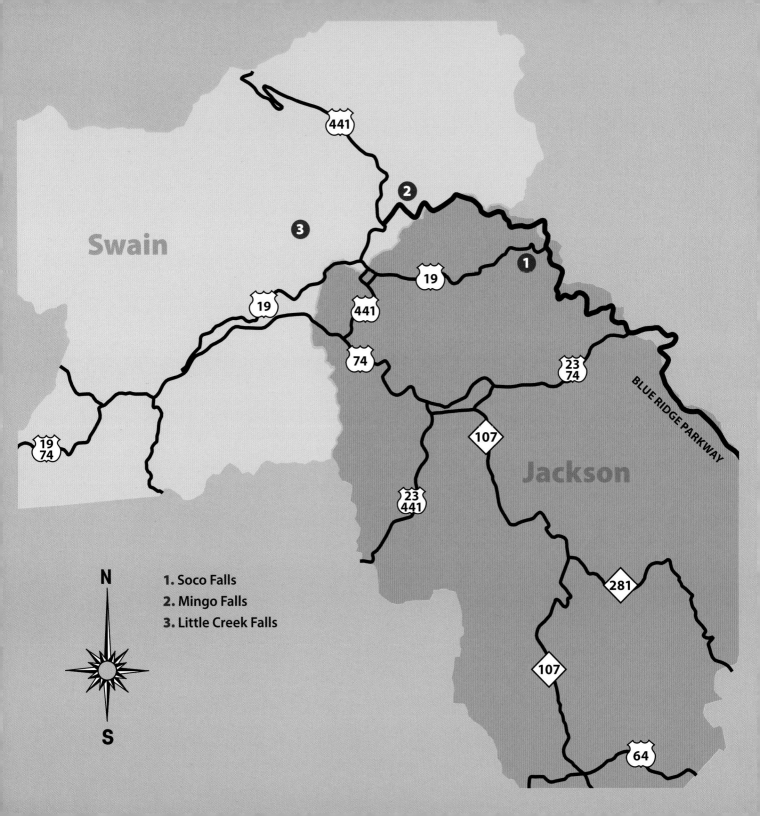

# Soco Falls

**Beauty:** 8

**Water Flow:** Moderate

**Height:** 35 feet

**Type:** Twin falls with cascades and free falls

**Property Owner:** Cherokee Indian Reservation

**County:** Jackson

**Trail Rating:** 3, 8 to base

**Trail Length (one-way):** About 100 yards to base

**Description:** An incredibly beautiful spot with twin falls forming a single creek at their bases. They are a series of short freefalls with near vertical cascades. There is a remote feeling to the location, although it is just below the highway. It is amazing that thousands of tourists pass by every year with no idea of the beautiful waterfalls just off the road.

**Directions to Trail:** The gravel pullout is located on US 19, 1.5 miles west of the Blue Ridge Parkway on the left. If you are coming from Cherokee, the pullout is on the right 9.3 miles from the Harrah's Casino Hotel entrance.

**Trail Directions:** The trail begins at the opening in the guardrail and winds down the bank to an observation deck. The view here is constricted and the right side waterfall is the only one clearly visible. If you want a good view of both falls, continue on the trail to the base, but be aware that the loose soil is very slippery and there is stinging nettle around the cleared area.

**Photographic Locations:** The right side fall can be photographed from the observation deck. To shoot both falls you will need to descend the steep and slippery trail to the base and shoot from just downstream. The spray from the falls makes it hard to get a good shots here that don't have droplets in the frame.

# Mingo Falls
## (Big Bear Falls)

**Beauty:** 9

**Water Flow:** Small

**Height:** Over 100 feet

**Type:** Steep cascades with short falls

**Property Owner:** Cherokee Indian Reservation

**County:** Swain

**Trail Rating:** 7

**Trail Length (one-way):** Just over 250 yards

**Description:** A very tall series of freefalls and near vertical cascades that drop to short falls and cascades towards the bottom. Although it is relatively narrow, it is indeed spectacular. Lush green forest borders the falls on both sides completing the breathtaking view. If you are in the Cherokee area, this waterfall is definitely a must see.

**Directions to Trail:** If you are traveling on the Blue Ridge Parkway, take it to where it ends at US 441 just north of Cherokee. Turn left on US 441 for 0.5 mile to a left on Saunooke Bridge Road. There will be a sign for Big Cove Road as many of the campgrounds in Cherokee are here. Take a left on Big Cove Road and proceed for just under 5 miles to Mingo Falls Campground on the right. There is a large paved parking area straight across the bridge.

If you are traveling north on US 441 from Cherokee, go past all the shops and the fairgrounds. Just after you pass the amusement park on the left, Big Cove Road will be on your right. There is a large brown sign pointing the way.

**Trail Directions:** The trail starts at the rear of the paved parking area and climbs up a number of stairs. The trail will level out and continue along the creek to a large footbridge that also serves as an observation area.

**Photographic Locations:** The footbridge serves as the best location for photographing Mingo Falls. You can shoot the entire waterfall with a vertical shot from here.

# Little Creek Falls

**Beauty:** 7

**Water Flow:** Small

**Height:** 55 feet

**Type:** Steep multi-level cascade with short falls

**Property Owner:** Great Smoky Mountains National Park

**County:** Swain

**Trail Rating:** 7

**Trail Length (one-way):** Just under 1.5 miles

**Description:** This is a nice looking waterfall of steep cascades and short falls over a layered rock face and is the one that adorned the cover of Mark Morrison's guidebook from 1999. The large log in the center of the falls was there then and still looks exactly as it did a decade ago.

**Directions to Trail:** From the intersection of US 19 and US 441 North in Cherokee, take US 19 west for 5.6 miles to a right on Coopers Creek Road (SR 1355). Continue on Coopers Creek Road all the way to the end at Cooper Creek Trout Farm. Check in at the office building and let them know you are visiting the falls or camping at the campsites. Just past the office, the road will fork. Go to the right and park in the small gravel parking area on the left just past the long cinder block foundation. Do not block the water intake structure on the right. The trout farm is open to the public from 10:00 to 5:30 daily but you may want to call ahead, especially during the winter. The owner, John Hunnicutt, is gracious and welcoming for those coming to see the falls. Their phone number is (828) 488-2500.

**Trail Directions:** Continue up the road and go around the gate. You will enter the GSMNP at the sign and blazed trees. The road will gradually ascend and pass a clearing on the right with campsites. The road serves as a creek bed in this section when Cooper Creek is high so rock hop or use the edge of the road. At about .75 mile, Little Creek crosses the road. There is a side trail to the left with a footbridge so you won't have to cross at the ford. Just past the creek crossing, the road forks. Take the road to the left and continue until you reach a footbridge that crosses Little Creek to the left. The trail narrows past the footbridge and becomes noticeably steeper. You will come to a switchback and then a long stretch before reaching the base.

**Photographic Locations:** The footbridge is the best location to shoot from. Be very careful here as the bridge is slippery and half of the handrail is missing. A vertical shot will capture this fall nicely.

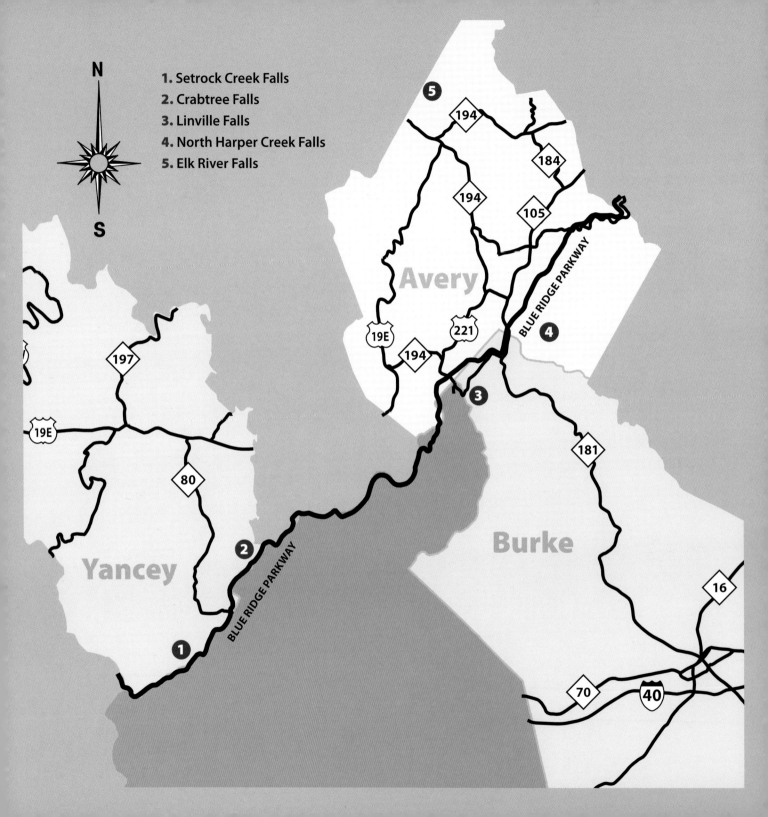

N
S

1. Setrock Creek Falls
2. Crabtree Falls
3. Linville Falls
4. North Harper Creek Falls
5. Elk River Falls

Yancey

Avery

Burke

BLUE RIDGE PARKWAY

BLUE RIDGE PARKWAY

197

19E

80

19E

194

194

184

105

221

194

181

16

70

40

# CHAPTER 9

# Mt. Mitchell, Linville, Elk Park

*Setrock Creek Falls*

*Crabtree Falls*

*Linville Falls*

*North Harper Creek Falls*

*Elk River Falls*

# Setrock Creek Falls

**Beauty:** 7

**Water Flow:** Very small

**Height:** 55 feet

**Type:** Zigzagging cascades and short falls

**Property Owner:** Pisgah National Forest

**County:** Yancey

**Trail Rating:** 4

**Trail Length (one-way):** Just over 0.5 mile

**Description:** This is an unusual waterfall that turns and drops over several ledges to a small pool at the base. The flow here may be very small but there is a lot going on from top to bottom at this fall.

**Directions to Trail:** Beginning at the junction of NC 80 and the Blue Ridge Parkway near Milepost 344, take NC 80 for 2.2 miles to a left on South Toe River Road (SR 1205). The road will turn to gravel FR 472 at 1.0 mile, and at 2.3 miles you will come to a 3-way fork. Take the far right road for 0.8 mile to a parking area with a map and information kiosk on left just before the entrance to the Black Mountain Campground.

**Trail Directions:** From the parking area, cross the bridge and enter the campground. Take Briar Bottom Road, the first gravel road on the left across from the campground office. Continue through the turnaround and trash bin area and take Briar Bottom Bike Trail that branches left. Keep straight when the Mt. Mitchell Trail turns right and continue across a long footbridge. Just past the bridge take the trail that branches to the right, continue across Briar Bottom Road, and pick up the Setrock Creek Falls Trail that begins at the stone steps. Trail will ascend gradually for about 200 yards to the falls. There are some roots and large rocks to deal with along this trail that can be slippery.

**Photographic Locations:** This is one of the hardest waterfalls to photograph. The canopy is open at the top of the falls and closed at the bottom. It has a tendency to glare out at the top and be dark at the bottom. It is essential to catch this fall under cloud cover if at all possible.

Anywhere on the rocks in the steam bed will make a good location for capturing the entire waterfall as will the left side of the creek or the area at the end of the trail. This fall looks nice with both horizontal and vertical shots.

# Crabtree Falls
## *(Upper Falls)*

**Beauty:** 9

**Water Flow:** Small

**Height:** 70 feet

**Type:** Very steep cascade with short falls

**Property Owner:** Blue Ridge Parkway

**County:** Yancey

**Trail Rating:** 7

**Trail Length (one-way):** 0.9 mile to falls, 2.0 mile loop trail

**Description:** An incredibly beautiful waterfall located in an equally beautiful setting. The relatively small flow spreads out over the many faceted, small rock ledges, producing a very unique look.

**Directions to Trail:** The trail to Crabtree Falls is at Crabtree Meadows Campground, located between Mileposts 339 and 340 on the Blue Ridge Parkway. Park in the paved area behind the small booth at the campground entrance. There are signs pointing the way once you turn off the Parkway.

**Trail Directions:** The trail begins at the trail map and information signs at the edge of the parking area. It descends to a T intersection where the loop trail begins. Go to the right for the shortest route to the falls. The descending trail is a fairly easy hike but there are a number of rocks and roots to negotiate. There are also a couple of places along the trail that also serve as a streambed so exercise caution on the wet rocks. There are sections of stone and timber steps that, combined with the somewhat steep trail, makes the return trip much more difficult. You can continue on the loop from the falls for just over a mile back to the parking area but going this way also gives you a good workout. If you decide to continue on the loop trail, keep left as you come to trails branching to the right. These trails go to the campground.

**Photographic Locations:** There are a number of great locations to shoot from here, beginning with the footbridge over the creek just downstream from the base of the falls. Anywhere around the streambed or to the right of the falls can produce great pictures, depending on whether you want frontal or profile shots. Horizontal or vertical views also work well with this waterfall. Be careful when walking on the slick, wet rocks and fallen trees.

# Linville Falls

**Beauty:** 9

**Water Flow:** Moderate

**Height:** 50 feet

**Type:** Upper drop to snaking cascade and two lower drops

**Property Owner:** Blue Ridge Parkway

**County:** Burke

**Trail Rating:** 4-7 depending on trails taken

**Trail Length (one-way):** 0.5 to 0.9 mile depending on trails taken

**Description:** Linville Falls is one of the most visited, popular, and interesting waterfalls in the state. It consists of a short upper fall with a nearly level cascade leading to lower falls that shoot out into the gorge. There were a number of trail scenes and an ambush scene filmed here for the major Hollywood film, *The Last of the Mohicans.* The falls, Linville Falls community, and the town of Linville are all named for William Linville and his son John, early explorers who were killed while camping near the falls by Cherokees in 1766.

**Directions to Trail:** You have two choices depending on where you're coming from. From the junction of US 221 and NC 183 at the small community of Linville Falls, take NC 183 east for 0.7 mile to a gravel road that bears right. This is Kistler Memorial Highway and the parking area is 0.1 mile on the left.

From the Blue Ridge Parkway, take the road to the visitor center and parking area that is located between Mileposts 316 and 317, one mile north of US 221. The parking area is just under 1.5 miles from the parkway.

**Trail Directions:** There are a number of well-marked trails here. They begin at either the visitor center or the parking area on the Kistler Memorial Highway. From the visitor center, you can take the left trail to Plunge Basin Overlook and Plunge Basin near the base, while the right trail joins the trail from the parking area. From the parking area, the trail descends to merge with the trail from the visitor center before coming to a T-junction at 0.4 mile. The trail to the left leads to Upper Falls Overlook, the trail to the right goes to Chimney View Overlook at 0.3 mile and Erwin View at 0.4 mile.

**Photographic Locations:** Linville Falls provides arguably the most locations of any waterfall in North Carolina for taking great pictures. My personal favorite for getting the best view of the falls, river, gorge wall, and surrounding scenery is from Erwin View.

# North Harper Creek Falls

**Beauty:** 8

**Water Flow:** Small

**Height:** 40 feet

**Type:** Long series of cascades with lower falls

**Property Owner:** Pisgah National Forest

**County:** Avery

**Trail Rating:** 7

**Trail Length (one-way):** 1.0 mile

**Description:** North Harper Creek Falls is a series of cascades over a long, sloping exposed rock outcropping ending in a near vertical drop at the bottom over a wide cliff into a small, shallow pool.

**Directions to Trail:** From just south of Milepost 311, 0.9 mile north of NC 181, turn south on SR 1518. There is no sign designating the road number but it is the only gravel road along this section of the Parkway. Proceed for 1.7 miles to Long Ridge Baptist Church on the left in a sharp right curve. Running alongside the church will be FR 464 (Edgemont Road). Take this gravel road for 2.5 miles to FR 58 (Kawana Road) on the right. Go 0.25 mile, crossing the one lane bridge to a pullout on the left at the trailhead.

**Trail Directions:** Beginning at the trailhead sign, the trail descends gradually and winds through the forest before coming to the first of several creek crossings. The trail is red and blue blazed until the second crossing, which is a bit tricky with a slick sloping rock, after which you will follow the blue blazed trail downstream. There will be two sloping rock outcroppings to cross, the second of which is steep and somewhat eroded. There are rocks and a log in place below it to shore up this section. Continue past the next two creek crossings, the second is made easier by two small logs placed over the creek. Just past the last crossing there will be a cleared campsite on the right. Turn here and cross the campsite to the creek, looking upstream for an area where the creek splits around a wide, flat rock. Cross here and pick up the narrow trail on the far side. It will widen out and descend gradually before becoming steeper after a switchback. The trail will come out just downstream from the base.

**Photographic Locations:** Along either side of the creek will yield nice profile shots, while the large rocks in the center of the creek just downstream from the falls is another excellent spot for frontal views. Horizontal shots work best here.

# Elk River Falls
## (Elk Falls, Big Falls)

**Beauty:** 8

**Water Flow:** Moderate

**Height:** 50 feet

**Type:** A concave, nearly vertical drop

**Property Owner:** Pisgah National Forest

**County:** Avery

**Trail Rating:** 5

**Trail Length (one-way):** approximately 300 yards

**Description:** An incredibly powerful drop over a concave shaped cut in a massive exposed rock cliff and into a large deep pool that makes a great spot for swimming. There will be kids of all ages swimming, sunbathing, and lounging on the rocks if you come on a hot summer day.

**Directions to Trail:** Elk Park, a small, quaint mountain town and not actually a park, is located on US 19E just before the Tennessee border. Once you get into town, turn right on Geter Oaks (SR 1378), which is 0.7 mile north of the NC 194 junction, and then take an immediate left on Old Mill Road (SR 1303). There are signs for both the falls and Elk Park Christian Church here. Proceed for 0.5 mile to a right on Elk River Road. If you should miss the turn on Geter Oaks, you can turn right on Old Mill Road which reconnects with US 19E after a short distance. There is a sign for the falls here as well. Then simply take a left on Elk River Road. Take Elk River Road for 4.0 miles to a parking and turnaround area. The road will turn to gravel at 3.8 miles where you enter the Pisgah National Forest.

**Trail Directions:** The trail begins at the parking area and gradually ascends timber and earth stairs to a relatively level grade. Trail begins a gradual descent to more timber and earth stairs down to a long rock outcropping at the outer edge of a large, deep pool. These descending steps and rocks can be slippery so negotiate them carefully to avoid falling. This is the part of the trail that rates a 5. It is otherwise a fairly leisurely hike.

**Photographic Locations:** Anywhere along the rock outcropping at the end of the trail will yield the best shots unless you want to get wet and venture into the river for additional angles to the left of the falls. Shooting from either side will allow you to incorporate the large rock face and surrounding forest while cropping out the sky, which is difficult to do with a frontal shot.

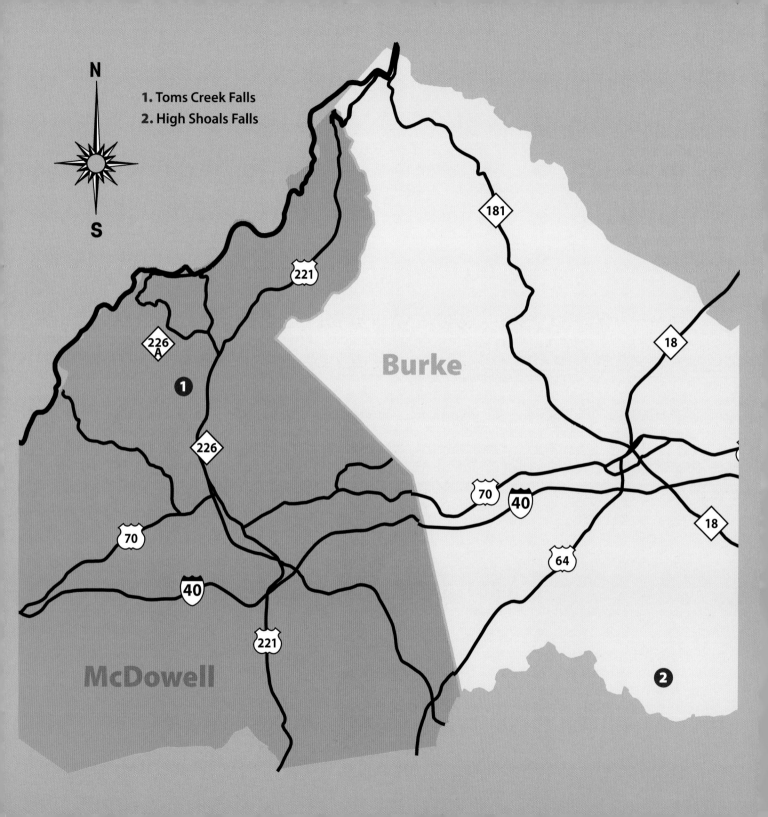

1. Toms Creek Falls
2. High Shoals Falls

N
S

226
A

1

221

226

70

40

221

McDowell

Burke

181

18

70 40

18

64

2

# CHAPTER 10

# Marion, Morganton

*Toms Creek Falls*

*High Shoals Falls*

# Toms Creek Falls

**Beauty:** 7

**Water Flow:** Small

**Height:** 60 feet

**Type:** Short falls and near-vertical cascades

**Property Owner:** Pisgah National Forest

**County:** McDowell

**Trail Rating:** 4

**Trail Length (one-way):** 0.4 mile

**Description:** A great looking waterfall that does a lot with a small flow. Short upper falls flow down to several ledges and continue with near-vertical cascades and short falls over a wide, moss-covered, layered channel carved out by the falling water over centuries. This one was a nice surprise, far surpassing any descriptions I had read about it, and well worth the effort to see it.

**Directions to Trail:** From I-40 you can take either US 221 north or NC 226 north at exits 85 or 86. Both will lead to an intersection with US 70 in Marion. From this intersection, take US 221/NC 226 north for 5.7 miles to a left turn on Huskins Branch Road. Take this road for 1.2 miles to a gravel parking area on the right. Huskins Branch Road will turn to gravel at 0.7 mile and back to pavement at 0.9 mile.

**Trail Directions:** The crushed gravel trail begins at the upper end of the parking area next to an information kiosk. It is wide and ascends gradually for most of the way. You will cross 2 small branches, one of which has a footbridge. Just before you reach the falls the trail will split. Take the right trail up the hill that leads to the base. You will be able to see the upper falls at this point.

**Photographic Locations:** Around the creek just below the base makes the best location for shooting here. The creek is shallow and you can move around on the rocks or the bank to get interesting angles or to include the surrounding foliage.

# High Shoals Falls

**Beauty:** 7

**Water Flow:** Moderate

**Height:** 50 feet

**Type:** Sheer drop with steep side cascade

**Property Owner:** South Mountains State Park

**County:** Burke

**Trail Rating:** 7

**Trail Length (one-way):** 1.0 mile to falls, 2.5 mile loop trail

**Description:** This is a very unique looking waterfall with a main drop of about 50 feet. There are small lower drops and a steep cascade flowing down the left side of the large rock face into a large, deep pool.

**Directions to Trail:** From I-40 in Morganton, take Exit 105 and make a left on NC 18 south. You will be following large brown directional signs for the park, but I'll give you directions anyway. Continue for 10.8 miles to a right turn on Sugar Loaf Road (SR1913). Take Sugar Loaf Road for 4.3 miles to a T intersection at Old NC 18. Make a left here and go 2.7 miles to a right turn on Wards Gap Road (SR 1901). Continue to a fork at 1.3 miles and bear right onto South Mountains Park Avenue (SR 1904). Park entrance gate is 1.1 miles. Proceed past the gate and park office for 2.3 miles to the Jacob Fork Picnic Area. Park here.

**Trail Directions:** The trail begins at the lower end of the parking area. The trails here are very well marked for direction and distance. The paved portion of the trail goes past a nice picnic area, a large map and information kiosk, and a cabin containing restrooms and a water fountain. Just past the cabin the pavement turns to an old dirt road that is wide and easy to hike. Continue to an open area with more kiosks that is the beginning of the loop trail. Keep straight until the trail forks and take the left trail for the straightest route to the falls. The trail narrows and you will begin to negotiate rocks and steps. There are a number of earth and timber steps on this trail, as well as stone steps. There is a nice splintered waterfall to the right of a long footbridge just below the main falls. My advice is to stop and admire the view and catch your breath here. You will need it as there are a number of steps from this point to the observation deck at the falls.

**Photographic Locations:** Anywhere on the observation deck will yield good pictures. Frontal and profile shots are good here. Horizontal and vertical views will yield good results.